You
Must
Relax.

You Must Relax

EDMUND JACOBSON, M.D.

McGRAW-HILL BOOK COMPANY
New York   St. Louis   San Francisco
Düsseldorf   London   Mexico   Panama
Sydney   Toronto

To My Mother

Book design by Stan Drate.

YOU MUST RELAX

Fifth Edition, Revised and Enlarged.

2 3 4 5 6 7 8 9 M U B P 7 9 8 7 6

Library of Congress Cataloging in Publication Data

Jacobson, Edmund, date
    You must relax.

    Bibliography: p.
    Includes index.
        1.   Relaxation. 2.   Stress (Physiology)   I.   Title.
RC351.J27   1976   616.8'04'5   75-33112
ISBN 0-07-032182-5

PREFACE

RELAXATION MAKES HISTORY

This is a tense world, as many of us well know. We talk about "tension" and we read about it. It is discussed in newspaper articles, in magazines and in books. Evidently, there is growing popular realization of something excessive in our way of living which can lead to disorder and malady. There is search for a remedy. Today doctors tell us to "relax".

This was not always so. When the famous physician who attended President Wilson wrote a book about rest, the word "relaxation" did not even appear in the index. People then did not discuss tension. The characters in movies written in that epoch did not tell each other to "relax" as they do nowadays, for the word had not yet sunk into the popular mores. I know, because ten years previously I had begun to develop the principles and the scientific study of tension and relaxation as we now know them.

I felt the burden of responsibility deeply. On the one hand I must test each advance in the field objectively, avoiding any enthusiasm which could cloud my judgment. Yet in my cold analysis as a scientist, I must not close my eyes to any light which could guide mankind.

My investigations were begun in the laboratory at Harvard University in 1908. Later I carried them further at Cornell and at the University of Chicago until 1936. Since then they have been conducted in a laboratory to which I have devoted my private means and my time, the Laboratory for Clinical Physiology in Chicago. The results of these investigations afforded practical measures for improving the health status of human beings. These practical measures have been tested and have been developed further over the years in my associated clinics.

My studies led to definite understanding of what tension really is—namely, the effort that is manifested in shortening of muscle fibers. Physiologists know this as muscle tension and have studied it in animals for over a century. I was attempting to begin where they left off in order to turn some of the vast basic knowledge which they had accumulated toward the benefit of man.

As I went along, I wrote up some of the results

and they appeared in scientific journals. Believing that the universal trend toward overactive minds and bodies could result in various ills, I wrote a book in 1929 called *Progressive Relaxation.* It was addressed to doctors and other scientists. Some said that it was very technical. Accordingly, the suggestion was made at the university that I write in simpler form for laymen. I did so under the title *You Must RELAX.* Since then many physicians have prescribed it as reading matter for their patients.

My path led through many difficulties. At first I had to contend with the fact that doctors and laymen alike were prone to think of amusement, recreation or hobbies at the mention of the word "relax".

Therefore I had to choose between (1) inventing a new word to mean neuromuscular relaxation and (2) trying to lead the public to use a word already familiar to them in the sense of recreation or hobby but diverted to mean neuromuscular relaxation. I chose the latter course. As the years have gone by, I have not regretted the decision. To an appreciable extent, the public has "caught on", and today the word "relax" has become part and parcel of daily speech in the sense of "let go" or "take it easy".

High nervous tension is prevalent in America today, leading to tension disorders of various types which will be discussed in this volume in an elementary manner.

What we know about the nervous system and the mind, what we know from investigation by electrical methods can be synthesized in one very important principle: relaxation is the direct negative of nervous excitement. It is the absence of nerve-muscle impulse. More simply said, *to be relaxed is the direct physiological opposite of being excited or disturbed.*

Is this obvious? I hope so, for I have worked hard over the years to make it become so. If it is even beginning to become incorporated into the thinking of the medical student, I am very glad. But let him draw the conclusions: nervous disturbance is at the same time mental disturbance. Neurosis and psychoneurosis are at the same time physiological disturbance; for they are forms of tension disorder. Thus whatever the psychiatrist accomplishes by his therapy, this accomplishment necessarily must consist in the diminution of neuromuscular excitability. And the success of any method used by the psychiatrist must be eventually in terms of the habitual relaxation that he has accomplished in and for his patient.

Tension is an objective manifestation of what all of us know in ourselves as effort. The same word is used not only for the effort which is in our every act, but also for an excess thereof. Thus, in one context, "tension" may mean reasonable effort in another, excessive effort. Once this matter is clarified, we can judge from the context whether the word "tension" is to be interpreted as meaning necessary effort or excessive effort.

In the newly added chapters I have tried to show more clearly how our efforts to achieve the smaller and the greater forms of success for which all of us strive can lead to tension disorders when these efforts become greater than our bodies can bear. But the aim of this volume is to preserve and to develop what is best in our efforts through a better internal organization. By learning to save ourselves physiologically we can take steps to prevent tension disorders.

Tension disorders include various common nervous disorders, including states of fear and anxiety, and they are often involved also in conditions known as peptic ulcer, nervous indigestion, spastic colon, high blood pressure, and coronary heart attacks.

The evidence indicates that our susceptibility to these conditions varies with our heredity as well as with the environment, including the pressures to which we are exposed. Taking into account all that is known today about the incidence of coronary heart disease, we cannot rule out the influence of heredity, for in the male, the lining of the coronary vessels is much thicker at birth than in the female, in whom the incidence of coronary heart disease is much less frequent. Fat deposits in this lining are believed to be increased by a diet rich in cholesterol. Individuals in whom tests show high blood cholesterol are advised to follow diets low in dairy products and other saturated fats.

In general we can say that coronary "heart

attacks" arise from coronary sclerosis plus tension. The greater the tension or the more advanced the sclerosis, the more likely the complication. We do not know all the causes of sclerosis, but evidence will be presented that tension favors its development.

This book, then, is written to teach people how to conserve their energies, thereby to avoid undue tension, yet ever striving for the success which seems to them good. Its purpose is to encourage them to take the advantage of the "built-in tranquilizer" which exists ready for use in every one of us. Why use sedatives and tranquilizing drugs with their many side-effects, asked my lifelong friend, Oscar G. Mayer—who originated the expression quoted—when nature has provided a built-in device free from all such defects?

To help in this direction of preventive medicine but also to train doctors and educators in respective fields of medicine and of education, there has recently been formed the Foundation for Scientific Relaxation. It is a non–profit organization. Thus it is a philanthropy which, in the opinion of its staff of businessmen, doctors and other scientists, can do much for the public welfare.

I realize that a popular book on common ills might prompt many to use it for self-healing when what they really need is diagnosis and instruction in the method of relaxation by a physician or some other form of medical attention. It is our hope eventually to have physicians trained in the field available to the public in various sections of the country.

However, scientific relaxation is not only a medical field. It is in addition a way of life. Today it is being taught in most university departments of physical education all over the country. Our field has become a part of undergraduate education. Furthermore, knowledge of scientific aspects is generally required of candidates for higher degrees in psychology.

EDMUND JACOBSON, M.D.
Laboratory for Clinical Physiology, Chicago

DIRECTIONS FOR USING THIS BOOK

This book is designed to help people cope with the difficulties and maladies of everyday life. It has two major and distinct parts. The first part describes the tension and tension disorders to which everybody is subject. The reader learns that his very efforts to cope are, in fact, expenditures of his energy, (his personal gasoline, actually his adenosine triphosphate) by which he lives, moves and has his being. He learns why success in living, like success in running a business, depends upon successful self-management, based upon thrift and upon knowledge of costs.

This first section credits "Nature" with the development of a wonderful living instrument, yet teaches that man needs to learn to run it efficiently for successful living. We cannot change our heredity, which unfortunately renders many of us susceptible to common maladies, such as high blood pressure and heart attacks; but we can learn to minimize hereditary maladies as well as those which result chiefly from different forms of everyday "stress".

This first section of the book, like the following section, is no mere theory, but is based upon sixty years of laboratory and clinical investigation from the standpoint of a cautious physiology and diagnostic medical practice.

The second section of this book instructs the reader by proved, practical methods how to run himself efficiently not only during the difficulties but also during the happy hours of life. He needs to learn how to run himself properly, just as he needs to learn to drive a motorcar properly. He will need to practice daily for best results, and directions in the book tell him what to do each day. He will learn that tension control has no exercises; for exercises are efforts. He will learn how to overcome costly habits of unnecessary effort-tension and will change to habitual easier living, saving in his daily energy costs while accomplishing what he really needs to do. He will learn to relax, thus avoiding tranquilizers, sedatives and hypnotics. By learning the energy thrift of differential relaxation, practiced in his daily duties, his amusements, his accustomed sports and physical exercises, he can learn to live more effectively, more pleasantly and possibly longer.

The writer is a scientist, respectful of the dedicated medical profession. Like other doctors, he knows that the public, when uneducated in medicine, tends to seek quick cures and panaceas. Learning to relax, as doctors know, cannot be achieved in two lessons, but wishful thinking can make it appear so. Progressive relaxation is the product of American science and cultivates self-reliance and independence, without reassurance and autosuggestions.

Acknowledgments

I am indebted for support and technical aid as long as I needed it to the Bell Telephone Laboratories, especially to Research Director Harold De-Forest Arnold, and to President Oliver Buckley and his successor, Mervin J. Kelly, as well as to electronics engineers H. A. Frederick and D. G. Blattner.

E. J.

CONTENTS

Section 2

Self-Mastery

The New Culture for the Troubled World

KNOW YOURSELF
TO SAVE YOURSELF

1

TENSION DISORDERS ARE MORE COMMON THAN THE COMMON COLD

In an advancing competitive society tension disorder tends to become the most common malady. During hard times, including inflation and loss of jobs, tension reduces personal efficiency all the more. No one today is justified in believing that he is free from tension unless present-day tests and measurements prove it.

In non-medical terms the cause of tension disorder is excessive effort. Efforts to overcome and to succeed are marked by complex patterns of emotional determination. Each person develops his own patterns of effort. Whatever the patterns, high tension results in symptoms and complaints familiar to every doctor, although not always correctly diagnosed.

Who are the contestants in this country in what has been called the "rat race"? During the past half century members of every common profession and business have come to my clinic with characteristic complaints, including lawyers, doctors, dentists, engineers, executives, reporters, columnists, editors, journalists, bankers and publishers. During the printing of my first book, *Progressive Relaxation*, in 1929, the printers and workers at the University of Chicago Press claimed that excessive tension applied *especially* to them. In later years, when I had the opportunity to meet with union members of the garment and other trades, it became evident that they likewise showed marked symptoms of high tension. The same held true for other workers. Certainly the assembly line is not a place where people can bask in comfort. Labor, like management, is marked by tense living.

Problems beset most men and women whether they are employees or run their own business. People often have trouble in getting along with each other. Wives and husbands do not always agree. Difficulties are encountered in raising children. Nowadays at school and at home, children have already begun to live tensely.

In short, whether the individual works in a factory or does housework or even lives a life of leisure, problems and difficulties continue to challenge the comfort we naturally seek. Even long vacations fail to provide an escape. Worries and fears obscure a clear future. Thus tension becomes a part of daily life. In the face of daily problems it is easy to become discouraged and sometimes overwhelmed. Too often effortful planning, with worried and fearful outlook, becomes a daily habit.

The complaints of people who have been living at high tension are many and various. Symptoms sometimes include fatigue and failure to sleep well. Drugs for insomnia are advertised on television, radio and other media. Still more publicized are antiperspirants. Excessive sweating is familiar to many people who live too tensely. The palms of the hands, the soles of the feet and the armpits are often moist. Obviously antiperspirants will fail to remove the cause and the customer will continue to sweat.

Often the tense individual notes a general bodily feeling of tension. It may appear to him in the chest, the back and/or in the arms. The back of the neck is frequently mentioned. Tension neckache is familiar and also tension headache. Sometimes tension is felt in the chest. There may be "uneasy feelings", perhaps fears, often in facing strangers or in speaking before people.

Experience has shown that high tension living can be responsible for symptoms and complaints from overactivity in each and every system of the body. The public should know that constipation and diarrhea often characterize high tension living. The constipation and/or spells of diarrhea may be intermittent or chronic. No statistics are available, but I conjecture that perhaps 90 or more percent of alimentary disorders result from overtense neuromuscular systems. As every physician knows, attacks of loose bowels often are attributable to gastrointestinal and other infections, including influenza, or to side-effects from drugs or to certain types of organic disease in the abdomen. What we are pointing out is that taken together, chronic or recurring diarrhea is much more often due to habitually high neuromuscular tension.

What is called "chronic indigestion" often results from general muscle overtension. Likewise, there may be frequent belching of air and passage of flatus. Sometimes there is mild abdominal discomfort, even pain. The doctor may discover "spastic colon" and properly attribute this to overtense living. He may call it "stress", a term I like to avoid because it has two very different meanings, one of which is unrelated to tension states. Burning sensations may occur in the upper abdomen. Bland diet and various types of antacids, mucosil, meta-mucil, Maalox and other preparations may relieve the discomfort, but neglect can lead the way to ulcer of the stomach or duodenum, conditions to which we shall return later.

Anybody with a history of ulcer may be sure that he has been and continues to be tense. Likewise anybody who takes tranquilizers either habitually or at times may be sure that he lives overtensely. Similarly the man or woman who smokes more than a package of cigarettes a day is far from being a relaxed person. The same applies to the man or woman who takes cocktails to ease down. Alcohol is an effective tranquilizing drug. Alcoholics invariably suffer severely from tension states. However, as is well exemplified in France, moderate drinkers may be no more tense than their less indulgent neighbors. Some moderate drinkers may be lured by pleasure rather than by need of tranquilization.

Many persons are driven to the doctor by "tightness in the chest", by fast and/or irregular heartbeats, by slight or marked discomfort in breathing, sometimes by hyperventilation. If an electrocardiogram is taken, it may be found "within normal limits". Thereupon the patient may become reassured and "try to forget it". Whether or not the patient is reassured, the chest and heart symptoms often point to high tension in his nerves and muscles, even if the doctor is pleased and discharges the patient as "normal".

Likewise if the electrocardiogram indicates some abnormality, such as early coronary insufficiency or more severe pathology, the patient can assume that he is too tense. Far from ruling out neuromuscular tension disorder, the heart findings definitely point to this malady as at least partly responsible for the organic heart disorder. This will be discussed later on.

"Tightness" in the chest with labored breathing is distress familiar to asthmatical patients. Fortunately, the symptoms can be abated with specific inhalant and other medications. There was a day when this was not so, and to save a life I was obliged to sit the night through teaching a new patient to relax the respiratory muscles. Even today, the asthmatic but also the elderly, emphysematous patient can gain by becoming adept at this skill. Likewise, in the treatment of chronic pulmonary tuberculosis along with specific medication at Veterans Administration hospitals, we should recall that doctors have applied progressive relaxation to further recovery.

Many people relate that their blood pressures often have been found high. This finding may be at times only. They may recognize that they become disturbed when their pressure is taken. Also, they may mention headache or even occasional dizziness. As we shall see, there is every reason why these people should learn to be relaxed in their daily lives. If the pressure has become chronically higher than normal, learning tension control is all the more necessary. In early hypertension, prevention is the aim of tension control medicine. In advanced hypertension, when surgery does not apply, we shall see why and how tension control methods can and should be applied with or without the concomitant use of antihypertensive drugs. Unfortunately, drugs are not cures.

Many and variable are other symptoms and behavior connected with being too tense. Some people speak of vague discomfort in parts of the body, often the back of the neck, often in parts of or throughout the back. Some suspect arthritis and visit the office of a specialist on rheumatism. According to the well-known orthopedist, Dr. Edward Compère, more than half of the patients who visited his clinic in Chicago with complaints of "arthritis" did not really have this disease but only some disturbing pains (personal communication). Accordingly, his treatment was to inform these patients that their chief malady was being too tense and he instructed them to read certain pages in this book. They were to practice as directed for two weeks and then to return to see him for further directions toward becoming less tense. He told me that generally he found this approach successful. Shortly after this meeting with Dr. Compère, I chanced to meet a surgeon who had been head of the surgical clinic of one of the leading Chicago hospitals. When I related to him the above-mentioned narrative, he responded that what was said would be understatement if applied to patients who had come to his surgical clinic. To my surprise it was his opinion that considerably more than 50 percent of these patients were in trouble chiefly because they were far too tense.

Tense women may suffer inordinately before and during menstrual periods. My gynecological experience, although limited, has suggested that some endocrine disorders for which hormones are commonly (and appropriately) prescribed can sometimes be treated instead by tension control physiology. Likewise with complaints from hyperthyroid conditions when not treated surgically. This field remains to be investigated.

Symptoms of psychotic maladies such as schizophrenic and manic-depressive states (cyclothymia) do not originate from high tension living but doubtless from hereditary abnormalities. The basic causes are as yet unknown and up to date are not corrigible.

Nevertheless, while high tension evidently is not the prime cause of these psychoses, it can play a role in the symptoms, complaints and treatment. There is much evidence that the success of any form of present-day psychiatric treatment of the symptoms of these psychoses can be measured by decline of tension states in the body neuromusculature. With patience, in psychotic depression the doctor who spends days in trying to discover the nature of a case of depression eventually will learn that the patient is worried and fearful about some matter which he visualizes at least intermittently. This is an example of ocular tension which requires the doctor's time to discover. Possible treatment will be outlined in a later chapter.

Readers interested in the symptoms and signs of tension during pregnancy, childbirth and thereafter will find a full description in the author's book *How to Relax and Have Your Baby*, published by the McGraw-Hill Book Company. As therein related, the first natural childbirth occurred in 1930 at the University of Chicago Hospital. Later Dr. Grantly Dick Reed read an early edition of *You Must RELAX* and spent years on promoting training to relax during labor for lessening of pain.

What shall we say of symptoms and complaints of "nervous" and neurotic ailments as related to high tension living? In my experience they are all characterized by measurable neuromuscular tension. In some neurotic maladies, especially hypochondria, the complaints and discomfort are incessant. When patients learn to cease complaining, hypochondria disappears. Yet this difficult malady in differing degrees is widespread among the populace!

"Nervousness" is the term popularly applied to a large variety of complaints, including worry, anxiety, fears and phobias. In past decades, the medical profession chose to class these ills as "functional"—i.e., without organic disease. A more recent nomenclature has been "psychosomatic". I doubt the precision of this terminology, since, as I have subsequently shown, there is no psychic occurrence in man which is non-somatic.[1]

Suffice it here to say that so called "functional" ailments all have characteristic neuromuscular physiology. In other words, what-

[1] In the Neurological Section of the American Medical Association meeting in 1921, I read a paper entitled, "The Use of Experimental Psychology in the Practice of Medicine" which was well received. This was the forerunner of the field later christened by someone else "Psychosomatic Medicine".

ever the form of the disturbing symptoms, they are structured in tension states. Accordingly, whatever reduces the tension states tends to reduce the symptoms, including the non-normal behavior. Readers desiring a better understanding are referred to my technical books addressed to the medical profession.

Although not scientifically proved, there is today strong evidence that *tension disorder as above described is more common than the common cold.*

Colds last but eight days and as a rule recur no more than about twice a year, while tension disorders remain with us the year round, particularly after adolescence. The predominance of tension disorders is indicated by statistics that tranquilizers are the most common of medicines. To this we should add the common use and abuse of the great tranquilizer, alcohol.

Tension disorders, as will appear farther in later chapters, have variegated manifestations often masked as digestive complaints, arthritic complaints, heart complaints and complaints of every system of the body, including the nervous and the mental. It seems not too much to say that tension disorders are the modern plague. United with inherited tendencies to specific systemic maladies as in high blood pressure and coronary insufficiency, they are responsible for our high death rates, as was cholera and other blights in former ages.

2

TENSE PEOPLE SPEND TOO MUCH ENERGY

Tense people spend too much of themselves. Their efforts are excessive instead of economical and efficient. They may succeed, but at unnecessary cost. When an effort is made for any purpose whatsoever, you contract muscle fibers in some combination. Effort is marked by successive patterns of skeletal muscle contraction. In general terms, your aim always is to achieve some reward or to avert some punishment. This is how you, the reader, and all other human beings live and move at every moment of waking life.

What is amazing in this modern age is the ignorance of humanity and the neglect by specialists in the life sciences of the relations of our purposes (motivations) to the mechanics by which they are carried out.

How is your purpose converted into your personal action? How is purpose related to body mechanics? We refer here to the mechanics of Galileo and of Newton, including the mechanics of present-day physics and engineering. Amazingly, this question has been neglected by all manner of students, including physicists and psychologists, philosophers and humanists. Nevertheless, until this question is asked and answered clearly, human thinking and human behavior will continue to be a mystery.

Purposes are carried out by contraction and relaxation patterns of the one thousand and thirty skeletal muscles which compose nearly half of the weight of the human body. Excepting in exercise, the muscle system as a whole has received little attention from scientists. When you contract muscles in your efforts, whatever your purpose, you spend personal energy. Tension (meaning nerve impulses with the shortening of muscle fibers) is your personal energy expenditure in carrying out your purposes.

Your automobile moves only if and when gasoline is burned to cause your wheels to turn. Likewise, a jet plane is propelled only if and when gasoline is burned to provide the energy for the engines. It is no different with your behavior and your thinking. These activities require fuel in your body to be burned in your nerves and muscles.

What is the name of the fuel you burn in your muscles, nerves and brain when you think and when you act in any manner whatsoever? It is named *adenosine triphosphate*, cyclic ATP for short. You should know this! You should be more familiar with this term than you are familiar with the word "gasoline".

This is because every moment of your effortful life depends on and results from the burning of adenosine triphosphate.

The discovery that all nerve and muscle cells depend upon this basic chemical has been due to the genius of cell physiologists. It is they who have studied individual muscle cells and fibers, their contraction and relaxation. They are physical chemists. Among other devices they have employed electron microscopes. To them I have been deeply indebted, and so should be our readers.

This is not to imply that they or other chemists have been interested in the whole man. Unfortunately, up to date you, yourself, have been neglected in your energy expenditures excepting when you engage in physical exercise.

Accordingly, we here depend largely upon what our own physiological laboratory and our own clinical studies have indicated about you in your daily efforts at work, at leisure and at rest. At every moment you depend upon your personal energy expenditures—namely, you burn adenosine triphosphate in your muscle fibers, in your nerve cells and fibers and in your brain cells and fibers. In this burning of fuel you resemble an automobile or a plane, which likewise burns fuel in order to move.

Different from these vehicles, however, the fuel you burn cannot be purchased. Instead, it must be manufactured from the food you have digested. This occurs without your knowledge and without your aid in "laboratories" within your body. Nature has provided such "laboratories" in every man and every higher animal.

Whoever opens a business generally knows or soon learns that he must keep expenses down or else close up. When this basic tenet is ignored, as in the cases of the Rolls-Royce and the Penn Central corporations, failure and bankruptcy are the inevitable consequences. Businessmen generally realize the necessity of at least breaking even. Profit margins are the basis of financial security.

Nonetheless, the same financially thrifty businessmen of America generally fail to appreciate the necessity of energy thrift in their personal lives. They spend their ATP as if the supply were inexhaustible. In ignorance, since doctors do not teach them, they follow the road that can lead toward exhaustion. I know, for I have had experience with the top management of some of the nation's most successful corporations. The officials conducted business duties with outstanding efficiency and success, yet spent their personal energies quite extravagantly. I was shocked to find that 40 percent of the top executives of one leading corporation had blood vessels that were beyond cure. They were paying with their lives for their years of energy extravagance.

While housewives as a rule are not trained in business, present-day high costs lead them to become economical. Not so of their energy costs. In my experience the American housewife commonly knows little about the necessity to conserve personal energy. In consequence of this ignorance and neglect, she often manifests some or many of the symptoms of energy extravagance recounted in Chapter 1.

Obviously, the guiding principle of business is and must be thrift. The same applies to finances at home and elsewhere. There is the same necessity to apply principles and practices of thrift to personal energy spent in the daily lives of everybody.

This is the lesson of the present volume addressed to everybody. We realize that it will require decades at least for people generally to develop habits of energy conservation even to the extent that they have learned financial thrift. However, in the last decade we have made notable progress, especially in American colleges and universities, where these principles now are widely studied and taught. Departments of education, especially physical educators, teach and apply the principles of tension control. Likewise departments of engineering psychology, as well as of clinical psychology commonly teach their students these psychological and physiological principles.

Slowly and doubtless inevitably we can expect these teachings to spread to other nations.

3

SUCCESSFUL LIVING

Open a business, spend your assets extravagantly, and what will happen? The answer is "You will go broke!" and the moral is "Control your expenditures!"

Why should anybody expect the opposite to hold true of personal energy costs? Common sense would say, "Your personal energy is your most important asset! Be careful of it! Spend it wisely!" But as we shall see, people generally use more common sense in business than in their living habits. For example, many have learned the value of physical exercise and of appropriate diet, but fads often prevail.

Most people have not even heard of progressive relaxation. They have not realized that at every moment they live by personal energy expenditure. Amazing to relate, this applies to millions of otherwise well-educated men and women! Many have not heard that energy costs in any person can be measured accurately today by laboratory instruments.

The busy doctor, however dedicated, may have little time to look up the literature on energy costs, much less to teach his patients.

Not knowing of scientific advances and usages, many people say that they "relax" by listening to music or by watching television or by reading or by playing golf. Such occupations would better be thought of as forms of amusement or of physical exercise. Properly speaking, they exemplify "recreation", not muscle relaxation. The word "relaxation" is used in this book as scientists use the word—namely, to mean discontinuance of muscle contraction.

However, learning to be habitually relaxed rather than tense does not mean to become lazy, any more than thrift in business means spending insufficiently. In this connection I recall a pleasant dinner to which I was invited by a very wealthy stockbroker, who wished me to teach a member of his family to relax. Instead of asking me questions, he gave me a lesson about relaxation training. With an air of authority he stated that to be relaxed is to be lazy.

The dinner table was no place to argue. Accordingly, I let it go at that. His millions from the stock market led him to feel authoritative about matters not related to his field of business. I have seen this overweening characteristic occasionally in other "self-made" businessmen.

How do you spend your personal energy? You spend it when you tense your muscles. Your muscles look entirely like raw steak from cattle. They consist largely of fibers that are long but often so thin that it requires a microscope to see a single one of them. In life, these fibers shorten whenever the muscle is used in whole or in part in any act of behavior or of thinking. This is called "contraction", or, if you like, "tension". Following contraction, muscles lengthen naturally. This is called relaxation. I like to call this natural lengthening "going negative", because no effort is required. *In fact, an effort to relax always is failure to relax.*

Why bother to learn anything about your muscle fibers? This question deserves a decisive answer. Think of driving a car without knowing how it moves on wheels! Think of flying a plane while not knowing how it is propelled! Such ignorance would be "startling" and "unnatural"! Now think of living all your life without knowing how you live and move and have your being. Is not such ignorance amazing in otherwise intelligent societies during this twentieth century?

In this brief book, publicly addressed, we can do little more than outline how you behave and how you think, based on current science, including particularly my own laboratory findings. As previously indicated, my aim is to give needed information about yourself in order to promote skilled, knowledgeable living, comparable with the skill and knowledge of the millions of people who drive motorcars successfully.

Simply stated, Nature, via evolution, has made you capable as a rule of surviving the trials and tribulations of daily changing environment. At each and every moment, for the benefit of yourself, family, friends and larger community interests, you make efforts. These are the tensions and relaxations of your muscles under nerve controls. At any moment of waking life your purpose (as previously stated in most general terms) is to seek some kind of reward and/or to avoid some kind of setback or punishment.

Obviously, your momentary purposes represent what you mean to do. The nature of thinking and planning is to engage in muscular action of such slight character that it is invisible. However, the patterns thereof can be precisely recorded with my integrating neurovoltmeter. This instrument measures muscle and nerve tension however slight. Thus it measures mental activity precisely, down to one ten-millionth of a volt. This has enabled us to prove that thinking at any moment occurs not alone in the brain but simultaneously therewith in our nerves and muscles. This is easy to understand by comparison with what occurs when we telephone. Not only does "central" operate to make connections, corresponding to brain action, but at the same moment we use our telephones at the periphery, as we use our nerves and muscles when we think. The thinking and planning becomes behavior when the muscle patterns increase in tension, becoming visible. Thus there is no big gap between what you mean to do and your subsequent overt muscular movements to do it. In other words, your behavior is only the subsequent muscular movements which are in accordance with the incipient patterns which characterize your thinking.

Nature has solved this problem for living creatures that have brains. It has interlocked purposes with internal forces which are unleashed to accomplish them, as I have epitomized above. Your brain-nervous-muscular system thus is an extremely complicated electrochemical-mechanical integrated system which operates in accordance with what you represent to yourself as what you had best do. No car and no plane is endowed with purposes. Their movements occur through mechanical controls. In contrast, your body moves purposively.

While Nature has thus provided man with controls, it has never provided him with the education needed to employ them knowingly. Indeed, for the most part, Nature lets man learn for himself. Society provides schools and other opportunities for learning. Accordingly, if man is to learn effective self-control, we humans must provide the knowledge and the facilities and we must show the way. That is the aim of the present volume.

4

TENSION AND HIGH BLOOD PRESSURE

In 1943 the directing doctors of the Metropolitan Life Insurance Company called me in consultation concerning accurate blood pressure determination. Their life insurance policies were based on the figures furnished to headquarters by their thousands of doctors who examined applicants in their homes and offices, including blood pressure determinations. They used the Baumanometer, a satisfactory instrument. I was questioned about possible improvements on instruments and methods.

In the course of this consultation concerning instruments and how their medical examiners could use them more reliably, the home-office doctors first learned of progressive relaxation and its possible application to blood pressure and coronary heart attacks. After looking into the subject, Dr. Charles L. Christiernen, the head of the medical department of the Metropolitan Life Insurance Company, concluded that at long last a medical approach had become available for the prevention and treatment of the cardiovascular disorders which were causing the highest death rate of all ailments in the United States. He formed a department of employees who suffered from these disorders to be treated by a doctor whom he sent to Chicago for training. He hoped to secure the interest and aid of other insurance companies. Unfortunately his untimely death and the onset of World War II ended his efforts. His insight still stands out, however. It has been confirmed by the statistics from fifty years of application of progressive relaxation method to patients with essential hypertension in two series—namely (1) without and (2) with the use of antihypertensive drugs. Modern instruments have been employed, including the ultrasonic apparatus and our integrating neurovoltmeter. All determinations have been registered by our Digital Computer, and scores of computerized graphs have indicated useful results. In Series 1, mentioned above, fifty-six patients received instruction and practiced daily in tension control. The composite graph determined by our computer showed a dramatic fall in the very first month. During subsequent months the averaged systolic and diastolic values continued to fall, but much more gradually. In Series 2 the results also were encouraging, especially since in many of the cases it became possible eventually to omit the antihypertensive drugs. We have reason to hope that in time doctors will include in their many other duties the teachings of progressive relaxation to their blood pressure patients, with and/or without the application of helpful drugs, as may seem best in each case.

Why does tension—why does increased burning of personal energy fuel, adenosine triphosphate—why do excessive efforts heighten blood pressure? Why expect otherwise? Inevitably, increased efforts indicate increased action in the neuromuscular system. Through central connections, the heart is stimulated to increased output per minute. Automatically, blood supply to the overacting muscles becomes increased. Thus oxygen supply to the overactive muscles is increased as needed, while increased pressure is reflexly produced to carry off waste products to be eliminated from the body.

This account is oversimplified. The basic mechanics of blood pressure increase are known to physiologists. Rise of blood pressure upon increased (effortful) muscular tension in tense patients and to a less extent in normal controls presently is measured almost daily in our Laboratory for Clinical Physiology. Many years have elapsed since this finding was first reported. Since then our tests have confirmed it over and over again.

For clarity, let me answer two questions: Is not chronic high blood pressure (essential hypertension) an inherited characteristic? Answer: We believe so. There is much evidence to that effect. Question: Then, why do you say that chronic high blood pressure is due to unnecessary, increased effort? Answer: I did not say that! I assume that the tendency to develop chronic high blood pressure (essential hypertension) is inborn but that the occurrence of dangerous levels can be and generally are stimulated by excessive effortful tension. Accordingly, preventative medicine is especially indicated in persons with bad inheritance. They should learn to save themselves.

Chronic high blood pressure can be due to abnormalities in the kidneys and elsewhere, curable by surgery, but in about 90 percent of the instances seen among our populace no such underlying malady is present. Since the cause has not been known, doctors have called the common variety "essential hypertension". In the early stages of this disorder, the blood pressure is elevated from time to time at least, but as yet little or no marked changes are demonstrable in the heart, kidneys or eye-grounds. Accordingly, many years ago I announced that the results in seventeen patients with early essential hypertension indicated that the disorder could be arrested in its progress and that the individual could learn to live in health.

I shall continue this chapter from a different standpoint—namely, with a heart-to-heart talk to those readers who have learned that at times at least their blood pressure is high and who have one or both parents with a history of hypertension. In my clinic we omit reassurance, doing better without it, since the patient learns self-reliance. Here, however, a few pages may serve to help individuals who are fearful, perhaps depressed over the future.

Any person who learns that he has high blood pressure has indeed something to worry about. But who has not? Our forefathers lived in times before humanity faced possible extinction from hydrogen bombs. Yet their favorite poet sang:

Be still, sad heart, and cease repining.
Behind the clouds is the sun, still shining.
Thy fate is the common fate of all.
Into each life some rain must fall.
Some days must be dark and dreary.

The poet's efforts may help a little, if only temporarily. In his day he did what he could to relieve sadness, depression and fear, emotions not then understood scientifically. His song, while beautiful, was primitive in its understanding of the human organism.

Man's very sadness is no merely poetical moment. Instead, it has many and various aspects. Indeed to be able to understand any emotion we must first understand the manifold nature of man, including his intellect.

Briefly let me say that at every waking moment there are certain purposes which you, the reader, endeavor to carry out, like every other developed human being.

You represent to yourself the outstanding features of the reality which concerns your interests and which you are meeting in your environment as well as within your own organism. You do this naturally, habitually and without realization that you do this.

Your representations generally include visual pictures at the moment in association with other kinds of images and in combination with muscular acts so slight as to be grossly invisible. However, I have recorded them with our instruments. Really, what you do at each moment is to estimate consciously what is going on of consequence to yourself. This is self-protection as well as purpose in life at every moment.

At each moment you appraise, using your voluntary muscles to begin to react properly. Simultaneously your intestinal and other involuntary muscles reflexly play their organic accompaniment much like the music which accompanies a movie. Thus you put emotion into each thought. Among these emotional accompaniments are tightening of the esophagus, which is the chief organ of our fears, although its digestive function is the passage of liquids and solids from the mouth to the stomach. When we become habitually overtense in our voluntary muscles, not only do we suffer excessive emotion designating our woes, but colitis, diarrhea and constipation become burdensome.

In excessive emotion, tension control is the answer. Psychiatry does not apply to colitis, diarrhea, constipation and digestive disorders, however emotional. Likewise, psychiatrists do not treat high blood pressure. Tension control is not psychiatry but is physiological self-engineering in which the patient, not the psychiatrist, is the dominant figure. The patient learns to become his own boss.

Accordingly, I hope that not only readers fearful of high blood pressure but likewise all other readers will familiarize themselves with the preceding paragraphs, so that they will understand the working of their minds.

In the second section of this book, instructions will be given for direct, efficient self-control, including mind and emotions.

5

TENSION AND HEART ATTACKS

A man of fifty for ten years had suffered pain and "tightness" in the region of his heart, generally lasting about an hour in each spell. Sometimes it began when walking against the wind or followed a heavy meal. Occasionally it awakened him from sleep at night. His business was selling paints at retail in a store which he had rented. He was not depressed but happily married, with two grown children. His father had died at sixty-three of coronary heart disease.

Most of the cardiograms during his past ten years had shown change from the normal. Upon examination I found his blood pressure somewhat elevated for his age. There were some minor ailments which I shall omit, since the present account will only be summary regarding his heart condition and is not intended to be a full case report.

After he had been examined, he received one hour of instruction in progressive relaxation at intervals of twenty-eight days, but printed cards informed him how he should practice one hour daily.

The pains were described as severe and crippling. Accordingly, I prescribed nitroglycerine tablets taken under the tongue three times a day. This helped him.

His improvement under instruction was very slow and was marked by relapses, but life became bearable and he missed no time at the store. Gradually it became possible to reduce the medication. After two years the nitroglycerine had been reduced from about sixty tablets per month to about twenty. No sedative, tranquilizer or medication other than nitroglycerine was used. It took him years to learn to be habitually relaxed in face of business and family worries, but he never had a coronary heart attack (thrombosis) and the chest pains diminished almost to zero. When last he was seen, after ten years of observation and oversight, nitroglycerine tablets were reduced to one or at the most two per twenty-eight days.

"My neighbor Harry is in the hospital. They say he has had a heart attack!"

Harry, perhaps, is a businessman well liked

by those who know him well. However, Harry could as well be disliked and he could be a factory worker, a lawyer, a doctor, an engineer, an admiral or any other type. Possibly he is forty-five or fifty years old or somewhat older, but he might be only thirty-five. There are many Harrys of many ages and this is one reason why I have written this book.

What has tension to do with Harry's heart attack? Let us first consider the case for the negative—namely, that tension has little or nothing to do with bringing it on. Many people, including some doctors and even some heart specialists, still believe this. Currently among these are some who assert that whether Harry has a heart attack or not depends on the state of his coronary arteries, whether these are hardened, sclerotic. Fat, they argue, is deposited in the heart arteries, weakening their walls, thus allowing them to burst or to develop stasis within, so that blood flow to some part of the heart-wall ceases, which is what people know as a heart attack. Arteriosclerosis, they add, is the cause of coronary heart disease and tension plays only a minor role if any. At most, it aggravates the symptoms, these polemicists claim, or sets off an attack through an emotional crisis, which would have come a little later on anyway.

Their arguments appear so sound, so scientific, so authoritative that we pause to wonder if they are not wholly right. Without doubt, fatty deposits are found in diseased coronary arteries. What, then, has tension to do with heart attacks? What, indeed?

There was a time when our boys were dying during the war in Korea. Three hundred of them died in combat whose hearts were carefully examined subsequently. Autopsies were performed by Major William F. Enos and his associates. Even though their age averaged in the early twenties, 77 percent had some degree of disease of the coronary arteries. In many instances, the hearts were so severely diseased that the examiners were amazed. They could not understand how these hearts had held out during the battle until the boy was killed by shot and shell or other external violence.

I do not know of any reasonable way to interpret the findings of Major Enos on these poor boys of ours but that the strain and tension of the war had proved too much for their arteries. Was it their diet? Did their hearts degenerate because they ate too much fat, too much cholesterol?

No record was found and published that could support the view that they had partaken of too much cholesterol. The Army diet does not provide any excess of fat. Nobody claims that it does. The fat content of meals provided for our Army forces was, we can assume, approximately of the same percentage as was provided for these boys in typical American homes in peacetime. So far as fat content was concerned, these boys had been eating as all Americans eat on the average.

Yet the incidence of severe coronary heart disease in these young boys was very much in excess of the incidence in American boys of the same age who had not participated in the strains and tensions of active warfare. It is said that approximately one out of two American males shows beginning hardening of the coronary arteries at the age of thirty-five or forty. But what is found in these early-middle-aged men is only the beginnings of disease, not advanced disease such as Major Enos found in many of our three hundred boys. And he found marked coronary heart disease not merely in one out of two but in the majority—namely, in about 77 percent.

The debaters therefore would find it hard to make out a case to prove that the coronary heart disease found in these fighters post mortem was due chiefly to fatty diet.

That dairy and animal fats often promote hardening of coronary arteries appears probable. Opinions and practices differ and the evidence cannot be reviewed here.

Perhaps I should indicate my own opinion if only to avert the impression that I am biased. I am not biased against restriction of diet for medical purposes. What is known as the salt-free or salt-poor diet was introduced into medical practice by an article on the subject which I wrote for the *Journal* of the American Medical Association in 1917. I restricted the fats in my own diet from

1912 to 1956. On the evidence I have not advised the same restriction to my family or to my patients, except where I have found blood cholesterol values high. My own values have never been high, and my restriction of fats was for prophylaxis only and on an experimental basis versus the ingestion of substances that might have some bearing on arteriosclerosis and carcinoma.

Incidentally, nutritionists fail to state that there are some people and many dogs who develop skin disorder on low-dairy and animal-fat diet. It can become serious, as in my own case. After I mentioned this in a lecture to Navy doctors many years ago, their outstanding cardiologist related to me his interest, stating that he had developed thus skin symptoms which local dermatologists had failed to diagnose.

Accordingly, we can return judicially to Major Enos and quite agree when he writes, "It is most unlikely that one factor alone can be indicated as the cause of coronary sclerosis". We can agree judicially while pointing out that the evidence for the importance of tension states is quite clear, if only the student does not focus exclusively on one factor alone, such as fat in the diet.

Major Enos concludes that the combatants suffered from *wear* and *tear* on the lining membranes of the coronary arteries and from *stress* at branching points. While he does not discuss the tense life at war as leading to the wear and tear and stress, his results contrast greatly with what we know of the normal, healthy hearts on the average in American boys in civilian life who have undergone no such strains. It seems safe to assume that their occupation as combatants with its extreme tensions of emotion and effort was largely responsible.

However, we are not yet finished with the matter. There is further reason to believe that students should not divorce tension from their explanations of the origin and development of coronary heart disease.

This is Harry's first heart attack, let us assume, in the sense that his doctor previously found nothing wrong in his heart record but now finds that the record indicates that the heart-wall has suffered damage. Nevertheless, Harry may have had heart pains previously, which were misinterpreted as digestive upsets or which were diagnosed as angina.

Doctors like to distinguish angina of the heart from coronary heart disease. Angina is thought of as merely spasm of the coronary arteries, through which the blood runs to supply the heart-wall, while coronary heart disease includes actual hardening and fatty change in those arteries, with resultant damage to sections of the heart-wall if, when and as the blood supply fails.

Angina means pain of a certain squeezing variety as a rule. In a later chapter I shall return to this interesting if gruesome topic. Angina may precede as well as mark the course of coronary heart disease in the form of spells, severe or light. In coronary heart disease, however, the pain may be absent or pass unnoticed. This is why people can die of it suddenly without previous warning.

Spasm of the coronary arteries (or any other artery) *is* tension therein. The circular muscle fibers are shortened persistently and excessively, and this *is* spasm. Throughout this volume, when "tension" is mentioned, it will always have a definite meaning, which may contrast with the vague usage found too often in current literature. Tension will mean the shortening of muscle fibers, which can be reversed. When reversed, the muscle fibers lengthen. This will be known herein as relaxation. All physiologists use the words "tension" and "relaxation" as defined above; at least they do so in their scientific work.

Heart specialists, including our debaters, are inclined to agree that among the causes of anginal spells are emotional episodes. None would be surprised even if the "organic" attack of Harry followed upon a severe argument with his boss at business, threatening the successful continuation of his career. But those who argue that tension has little or nothing to do with the real causation of Harry's diseased arteries claim that the basis of the disease was already there before his trouble with his boss. In this they are doubtless right. When we point out the apparent significance of tension in the development of coronary heart disease, the argument for this offense does not assume that tension is the one and only cause but only that it evidently plays a role that has been too much neglected. The traditional view of authorities generally has been that coronary heart disease, like arteriosclerosis in general, is of unknown origin, and therefore for the present at least we can do little to prevent it. I take issue with the traditional view because I believe that with better understanding of the role of tension we can do very much to prevent the incidence of coronary heart disease and at the very least can postpone attacks.

This opinion was shared by Dr. Charles Christiernen, chief physician of the Metropolitan Life Insurance Company when that organization began to take interest in the field of tension and relaxation methods some forty years ago. He became convinced of the magnitude of the role of tension toward developing coronary heart disease with its prime position among cardiovascular diseases as killer number one among the yearly deaths of our population. And as he learned more, he came to believe with me that the key to diminishing this high death rate lies in promulgation among the populace of technical methods of relaxation.

This is why: Without doubt organic characteristics in any individual determine the degree of his susceptibility to any disease, including coronary heart disease. If you are the offspring of two rabbits, there can be no doubt what you are.

Inevitably your heredity identifies you and marks you individually for life from all other living creatures. You inherit millions or billions of characteristics, which among other things determine your resistance to heart attacks.

But against every negative there is a positive. What brings on the disease? We cannot yet answer this question in all aspects definitely. But we can throw light on it by comparing our organisms with any man-made instrument or machine. We know that all of these are subject to wear and tear. We can consider what is to most of us the most familiar of machines, the automobile. Cars are turned out at the factories differing in the strength and resistance of their parts. Therefore some suffer damage more than others upon a collision. But in any accident the real cause of the damage never can be found solely in the materials. As a rule much depends upon the manner in which the car was driven. From our familiar experience with damage to cars in collisions, we can learn that the materials in a car do not usually suffice to explain the nature and extent of damage sustained in any collision. To explain the damage we must take into account also the nature of the driving or use of the car, whether good or bad. Sometimes poor driving can account for the chief features of the damage sustained. At other times poor materials may explain the chief features, as when a weak or loose fender is knocked off when one car chances slightly to scrape against another.

We must learn to take into account, then, not only the materials but also how we handle our cars, if we would minimize collisions and their ill-effects. Likewise in accounting for any disease, including heart disease, the modern doctor will no longer focus his attention exclusively on our material make-up, whether derived from heredity, diet or other means, but will consider also how we handle ourselves. His reason and his success will thereby be improved. For as we shall see, proper handling of ourselves is the avoidance of undue tension, provided that we live normally otherwise.

By avoiding undue tension, we can do what within us lies to prevent coronary heart disease or at least to slow its development. By conservation of our muscular energies we can save our hearts.

6

WHAT ABOUT STRESS?

Since I was one of the earliest investigators in the field known to most as "stress", it seems fitting that I say something about it here, particularly because the subject needs clarification.

Indeed the first laboratory studies in the field of stress were made in the Harvard Psychological Laboratory in 1908 and later appeared in my doctoral thesis on Inhibition (Cambridge, 1910).

In these studies I produced momentary stress in each subject sitting quietly in a quiet room with his attention on reading matter or some simple object such as a coin. The stress came suddenly, being produced by a very loud bang of a wooden slat against the top of a wooden table, startling the subject. I found that he moved violently and that this phenomenon could be repeated as often as eight times per hour. Only after I had taught him to be somewhat relaxed did this movement diminish or disappear. It is of course anything but pleasant to be so startled.

In 1925, under my direction at the University of Chicago, these earliest examples and measurements of momentary "stress" were continued by Margaret Miller in her studies toward the doctorate. To produce the "stress", she fired a gun as unexpectedly as possible under the laboratory conditions.

The term "stress" was used little or not at all in those early days. We can define the term in retrospect as signifying whatever stimulus or irritation is followed by nervous and/or mental disturbance. Today, this sense of the word "stress" has been extended to cover disturbing stimulus or other irritation in daily life to systems other than the nervous system, including the endocrine system.

Unfortunately for clear thinking, *a second and quite different type of physical disturbance* has been called "stress" in more recent decades. Confusion has been piled on confusion especially because workers in the field often have failed to write that thus there are two different meanings of the term "stress" in articles and books written for technical students as well as in others for the general public. In fact, articles for the general public have appeared not only in popular magazines but also in daily newspapers, adding to public confusion about so-called "stress".

This second and different field and meaning of "stress" is readily defined. Examples of this second meaning of the word "stress" are severe burns of the body, severe frostbite, severe hemorrhage, severe surgical operation or bodily injuries, severe bodily changes as when produced by flying at several times the speed of gravity. In this second sense of the word "stress", local injuries can sometimes be so termed.

By now our readers should clearly realize that there are two highly different meanings of the word "stress". So far as I know, this difference, this ambiguity of the term, has never been pointed out except in my own publications. It is time that medical writers in magazines and in newspapers become aware that the term "stress" is used in two greatly different senses.

Let me clarify further. Eminent scientists, including Professors Dwight Ingle and W. E. Sawyer, have made contributions to the field of "stress" in sense number two. These have been significant, educational and, I believe, beyond criticism. They have not always agreed with Investigator Hans Selye of Canada, but their disagreements do not concern us here, since the severe bodily injuries which they call "stress" are not included in the field of tension disorders and are not curable by progressive relaxation. Obviously, we do not believe that the damage in people who have been burned severely, who have been frozen in parts or who have suffered from severe hemorrhage or automobile injuries—we do not believe that in such injuries the damage is due to excessive muscle tension. Such a view would be irrational. There are many maladies different in symptoms and in body disabilities with little or no relations to tension disorders and which cannot be cured by progressive relaxation. Among these maladies unrelated to tension disorders are the various forms of severe body damage known to Ingle and Sawyer and Selye as "stress" (sense number two).

I hope and trust that the reader will now understand why I prefer to avoid the use of the word "stress", and I hope that he will join in promulgating clear thinking on the confused topic.

7

THE HIGH COST
OF ANXIETY

Anxiety is not limited to older people. It occurs at all ages. During World War II a number of cadets under training for the air arm of the U.S. Navy showed signs of strain, including instances commonly called "nervous breakdowns".

It was no wonder. Abrupt changes in life can be hard to bear. Fresh from their homes and their schools, youths of nineteen to twenty-two were being disciplined to fly and service planes for purposes of war against the Germans and the Japanese. At times they were exposed to dangers new and unfamiliar. The future offered little security. Yet there was no choice. Retreat to home was impossible, unthinkable.

To meet the problem, the U.S. Navy sent five officers, mostly of commander rank, to the Laboratory for Clinical Physiology in Chicago to be trained as instructors in scientific relaxation. They were not doctors, and therefore there was no design to prepare them to treat nervous illness. Besides the strictly medical department in the field of scientific relaxation which is for doctors and for doctors alone, there is also a department for educators. Good teachers in our schools and colleges, we believe, could do much to improve our daily habits of living. However, they must have received preparatory training in scientific relaxation. Navy authorities evidently understood.

Because of war urgency, an intensive course of training to be teachers was provided for the "Navy Five", as they called themselves. They could afford only six weeks time in Chicago. Hours for lectures and discussion were quickly arranged so that they could know what were the purposes and objectives of the training course and how they could teach the cadets effectively. But scientific relaxation is not just lying down or sitting up in quiet manner with good intentions. It is as technical an undertaking as running a plane, which many of the cadets were striving to learn. Accordingly, on each day of their course except Sundays, in three different periods lasting one hour apiece, the Navy Five were trained to relax. In some periods they lay on couches; in others, however, they sat up or they stood. They needed to acquire skill in relaxation themselves in order to transmit such skill to others.

But to acquire technical skill of any kind generally requires not only professional instruction but also practice on the part of the pupil. Accordingly, into a day already full, we had to crowd two additional hour periods for them to practice on what they were being taught. Furthermore, we had to provide for tests to know whether they were really learning.

For this I had designed electronic apparatus. I had been very fortunate in having the benevolent cooperation of the Bell Telephone Laboratories in this difficult electronic field and was greatly indebted for this to Dr. Mervin Kelly, the president, and to his predecessors in this office.

One hour per day was provided for testing how relaxed each of the Five was becoming. The tests showed that they were really learning.

Five or six hours per day of rest with muscles really relaxed, following a night of sleep, is a lot of rest for any healthy person, and therefore a balance had to be provided. This was especially necessary since the Navy Five were rugged athletes, some of them athletic coaches of national fame. We needed to keep up the daily exercise which had long been their habit. Therefore, at least once a day, each of the Navy Five engaged in vigorous athletics at the local YMCA. Thus they developed fatigue products which enabled them to relax more readily during the training hours in the laboratory.

They learned, however, that physical exercise has little relationship to technical relaxation. Athletics, we can agree, need no justification; they are part and parcel of a vigorous and healthy life. But relaxation skills are as applicable to the habits of sedentary people as to athletes. These skills have to do not only with the muscular exercise visible in athletics but quite as much with the invisible muscular activities which constitute our daily efforts. Until this is widely understood, many people will identify relaxation skill with physical exercise or the results. According to my experience, those who preach "relaxation exercises" have not quite understood that to relax is simply *not* to do; it is the total absence of any muscular exercise.

Understanding these matters, the Navy Five returned to the preflight schools in various parts of the United States. They trained ninety-five other officers to be teachers, making a total of one hundred relaxation officers. Within a period of the first seven months, 15,700 cadets received training. The results were published by Commander William Neufeld in the *American Journal of Psychiatry*. He reported evidence that, as a consequence of training, states of nervousness and fatigue were reduced in incidence, sleep was improved and accident rate lowered as compared with groups who had not received relaxation training. There was considerable enthusiasm among many who had participated as pupils but also among untrained officers and others who had the opportunity to observe the cadets.

Thus, according to the evidence, anxiety among cadets was on the whole diminished. Even so, they continued at their daily training to fit them for air combat. What can we learn from this and other studies as to the real causes of anxiety?

Popular opinion has it that anxiety is created by whatever troubles us. Thus a man whose position is in jeopardy may be deeply concerned about his prestige and about supporting his family. Or a mother may worry about the illness of her child. Similarly, according to popular opinion, the anxiety of the cadets was *caused* by the dangers, present and future, in learning to fly for combat.

Like many other popular views, there is some logical basis for the prevalent opinion that anxiety (where it does not concern personal health) generally is caused by external circumstances and situations. If I am startled upon the occurrence of a sudden noise, there is at least a partial justification for the belief that the noise caused the jump which I exhibited. If the noise had not occurred, I would not have jumped. But a scientific study disclosed that people are less startled or not at all if their muscles are generally relaxed. The individual exhibits the jump or startle reaction only if and when he is tense. What really happens, therefore, is that the startle merely is touched off or triggered by the noise. The noise acts as stimulus only, and there is a great difference between *stimulus* and *cause*. The cause of the startle or jump thus really is in large part the tenseness in the individual. When he is not tense, he is not disturbed by the noise emotionally.

If this is true, people generally have labored under a partly false impression about their concerns, fears and anxieties. Attributing the onset of these states solely to situations which are met, to the hardships or future hardships of life, has been a great popular mistake, which needs to be corrected in the interests of better living.

Ministers, priests and rabbis agree that without hardships such as lead toward anxiety, life would be drab. To meet trials and tribulations develops courage and character. It can make for higher spiritual development. Yet, this view, to which I heartily agree, does not go along with the view that the same trials and tribulations are the causes of our concerns and anxiety; for if they were the real causes, there would be nothing that we could do about our conduct. We would be the slaves of the situations which confront us.

I must confess that to a large extent people act as if they really were slaves. Their false beliefs confine them in intellectual concentration camps. But there is a way out to freedom, whereof I would speak in the present volume.

Let me illustrate. But yesterday I was met by a

man whose respect for the golden rule has been voiced and demonstrated in his business life. Yet he was emotionally upset, concerned over criticisms of his conduct, which led him to consider suicide as an escape and which led a psychiatrist to suggest a three-month stay in a mental hospital.

He regarded the criticisms leveled against him as the *cause* of the emotional disturbance which his facial expression revealed. Obviously, if these criticisms were really the cause, there was nothing much he could do for himself to improve his emotional condition. He was helpless. Therefore he thought of suicide, and the psychiatrist thought of shock treatment.

But there *was* something he could do about it. The first step was to correct the false belief which held him helpless. The situation which he faced was really unpredictable in its possible developments. No one could prophesy whether the future really held the ill for him which he feared. What he needed to do first of all was to appraise the situation objectively.

However, an overtense person tends to be ill-qualified to render objective judgments about matters over which he is disturbed emotionally. He fails to display what is known as the "judicial temperament". As he becomes relaxed, in my experience, his reasoning about such matters tends to improve. He sees things in a colder, clearer light.

How does the method of relaxation apply to

conditions of fear—normal or abnormal? The answer can be illustrated by the case history of an attorney who, in 1929, at the age of thirty-three, had already lived the modern life of rush and had amassed a small fortune following protracted hours of attention to business. He complained that in so doing he had "burned himself out"—had permanently impaired his vitality. Fatigue was frequently present, but, above all, "fears", as when speaking at court or when in high buildings.

It is not considered sufficient for such a condition to learn to be relaxed merely when lying down. Rather, it seems necessary for the patient to learn to recognize when and where he is tense during fears and to relax the localities involved. This is *differential relaxation.* Accordingly, this patient, after he had learned to relax very well lying down, as shown by electrical records, was trained to relax while sitting. His powers of observation were cultivated until he became able to report—without leading questions—what experiences he had at moments of fear. He said, for example, that when near a window in a high building, he had visual images of himself jumping out, along with tensions to look toward the window, but also with tensions in the limbs as if to withdraw. Assuming that his observations were substantially correct, he was instructed to relax all such tensions, including those of withdrawal, at the moment of fear. At first he complained that his relaxation was not quick enough. During treatment, without letting him know why, he was repeatedly instructed to imagine various objects falling and to report his experiences each time. For examples in succession: a magazine falling from the desk to the floor; a book falling from the windowsill to the floor; a small piece of plaster falling from the ceiling to the floor; a pebble falling out of the window. In the course of months, according to his reports, he developed an increasing control of those tensions. In 1933—two years after concluding treatment—he stated that he no longer had "fears". It seems important to note that his habits of working all day and long into the evening as a rule were not discontinued even during the period of treatment. He stated that he had become able to work more effectively by relaxing differentially. There was objective evidence that his fears subsided, since, following his course of treatment, he calmly moved his business to a desirable office space located in the tower of a high building.

The treatment described in the foregoing two paragraphs occurred in 1930. It effected lasting recovery in the attorney with no recurrence of phobic anxiety. He practiced law successfully, reaching the age of seventy-three, when he died of carcinoma.

More recently the method which eradicated the fearful impulses in the attorney as above accounted has been termed "desensitizing treatment". This appellation and the current popularity among psychiatrists of progressive relaxation applied to "desensitize" has issued from the teachings of the distinguished Professor Joseph Wolpe, Chief of the Department of Psychiatry at Temple University.

Professor Wolpe continues to train many psychiatrists in briefer applications of progressive relaxation methodology to nervous and psychiatric conditions.

If we are eventually to succeed in teaching tension control to many people, as seems most important, it becomes obvious that whatever time we can save for practitioners will be beneficial. Accordingly, abbreviated applications of progressive relaxation teaching constitute a most desired attempt at procedure by Professor Wolpe and his many trained psychiatric teachers.

Abbreviation of the doctors' time has been accomplished to a certain extent in my own clinics. In recent years, most of my patients in Chicago and New York have received one hour-long teaching treatment per twenty-eight days. This has become practical only through providing each patient with printed instruction cards the use of which indicates to him precisely what he is to practice each and every day between treatments.

This procedure has applied successfully not only to psychiatric cases but also to cases of essential hypertension, coronary insufficiency, spastic colon and the other varieties of tension disorders listed in Chapter 1 of the present volume. Obviously, essential hypertension could not be successfully treated by six or seven or some such number of periods.

It is pertinent to emphasize also that my teachers are trained so far as possible to avoid the use of suggestive therapy, including encouragement. We realize that both general practitioners as well as most specialists in all departments of medicine generally add words of suggestive encouraging therapy, more or less automatically. We try to avoid this on the ground that we are teaching independence to our patients and healthy pupils. We regard freedom from dependence on the doctor as among our most significant aims. To be sure, we realize that in every form of therapy there tends to be some contamination of therapeutic suggestion. We realize that we cannot achieve complete absence of therapeutic suggestion any more than our homes can be kept spotlessly clean. But following this analogy, there is a vast difference between a clean and a dirty home. Likewise we assume the cleaner we can keep progressive relaxation methodology from therapeutic suggestion, the more effective and lasting our results.

Let me illustrate again, this time with a married woman whose anxiety was not reasonable, as was that of the man mentioned, but in fact was so unreasonable as to indicate mental disorder. For several years, she related, she had been severely depressed over her "life-span". Worry had consumed her energies, both day and night. She was fifty years old, she said, and she could not endure this. Her life with her husband was successful. Their circumstances were less than comfortable; but they managed to get along.

To become fifty years old obviously is part of the normal state of healthy man and woman. You are not then what you once were; but if this stimulates you to unceasing worry, presumably there is something wrong with you rather than with your span of life.

The woman in question (whom I shall call Mrs. Hardy) said this of her own initiative. Other women were fifty and did not worry about their span of life until they became unfit for household and social duties, as she did. Therefore, she added, there certainly was something the matter with her mind. She knew that her anxiety was foolish, unreasonable, but she "could not stop worrying". She "must be headed for the psycho-pathic hospital!" What would become of her and her family? What did the future hold? She wept miserably.

Was this what is called a mental disorder of the menopause? Perhaps. However, it had not begun when menstruation ceased and did not have certain earmarks of menopause psychosis, as I know them.

In either case, what is the cause of such depression? The question as thus worded assumes that there is just one cause. This assumption generally is not justified when one deals with disorder in so complex an organism as the human.

If the question means, "What was wrong in her brain or elsewhere in her body?" it is a good question and deserves a straightforward answer. Her condition was diagnosed as cyclothymic depression, a term which means recurring spells of irrational depression and/or of mania, the cause and underlying pathology of which has not yet been established. We can investigate for possible metabolic or glandular disease, brain defect or other insufficiency, but as yet we do not know. We recognize that it is an inherited malady, more resistant to treatment than any tension disorder. Until the cause becomes established, it has seemed valuable to teach tension control if and when the patient could be induced to learn, including daily practice. Fortunately experience has taught me the means and technique toward reduction of symptoms of different types of anxiety states, whether rational or irrational, if the patient can be induced to cooperate. For this, thanks are due to specific relaxation methods, but an individualized approach is obligatory if there is even mild irrationality. Severe irrationality is not approachable by teaching methods. Obviously cyclothymic depression is not a tension disorder, although always characterized by severe tension symptoms and habits. When a lasting result is secured after prolonged progressive relaxation procedures, I surmise that the favorable result is due to our affording "nature" an improved opportunity to correct the underlying disease.

By these means, Mrs. Hardy was instructed step by step to recognize when and where she was tensing muscles at each moment of her life. She practiced faithfully and became expert at this art of recognition. Gradually she learned to distinguish between what she was tense about (i.e., her age) and her tension. Her tension could be felt by her variously in the sundry parts of her body. When she was particularly depressed, she could note a characteristic "heavy" feeling in the chest and abdomen, affecting breathing. She learned to recognize the sensation from muscle contraction when it occurs in any region in an arm or leg, in the trunk, neck or head by methods described in the second section of this book. She employed this sensation as a criterion for recognizing tension, somewhat as a shopper takes along a swatch or sample of a color of cloth which she wishes to match in a larger piece for purchase and use.

Thus learning, the day came when she began to realize that her life-span would not trouble her if she were not excessively tense. When troubled, she now became able to notice when and where she was contracting muscles, being tense unnecessarily. Her efforts to adapt herself to her daily responsibilities were found to be extreme. She was trying so hard that she really failed to meet her life situations successfully.

Accordingly, she practiced at being more relaxed not only during periods lying down but also during her housework, during her communications with family members and others as well as during her entire daily life. She learned step by step how to relax differently.

Thus she saved her energies.

Specifically, she learned that when she engaged in anxiety about her age and life-span, she was no mere puppet obliged to perform this act by external mechanical or other forces. On the contrary, although she had not been aware of it, it was she who had been actively performing in a manner which could have but one result—namely, anxiety.

She learned from her own skilled observation, once this had been developed, that at any moment of anxiety, *it was she doing*. She was doing something with her muscles just as definitely as if she were sweeping a room or washing the dishes. Anxiety was an act which (at least in part) she was performing but need not perform.

She was helped to realize this in moments when she had become relatively free from tension in her muscles. This occurred for the first time when she was lying down in practice. To her surprise, perhaps, for the first time in years she found herself free for the moment from the severe anxiety which previously had oppressed her constantly.

To her it was an amazing experience! For the moment and briefly thereafter it afforded her insight and a certain degree of hope. But in the disease from which she suffered, hope is an uncertain light. It flickers and is soon extinguished.

The doctor must know this and, oddly enough, should be careful not to speak to one with such disease encouragingly. Like a child suffering from inanition—perhaps dying, but unable to partake of the nourishment he needs—so the psychotic depressive tends to react with more depression to any marked encouragement offered in speech.

With little or no encouragement, therefore, but prompted to practice, Mrs. Hardy learned to save her muscular efforts to solve problems about her age. She came to realize that the greater her efforts to solve these problems, the worse was her condition. She had meant well; her intentions had been good. But, as she was informed, the adage applied to these efforts was "Good intentions pave the road to hell!"

By learning to go negative in her efforts to solve her problems regarding her advanced age, she gradually acquired insight, confidence and self-control. She became free from the fears that had held her a slave. She became confident, self-assured and cheerful. Measurements of her tension state confirmed her improvement by objective tests. She returned fully to her household duties, sustained financial trials with emotional calm when her husband met with financial difficulties and became able to help him in his business. It was believed that she now was free from nervousness, to a degree never before seen in her, even during younger years.

How can I explain so striking a result when I do not claim that research has as yet enabled us to understand the body state in cyclothymic disease? The interpretation seems to lie close at hand. Whatever the disease, whether we understand it fundamentally or not, saving our energy should in principle enable us to withstand it more successfully. This was accomplished in the case of Mrs. Hardy.

The moral of this chapter is: DON'T WEAR YOURSELF OUT!

8

ANXIETY AND ULCERS

In the public opinion, anxiety is closely linked to ulcers of the stomach and adjacent intestine. However, I know of no proof that this variety of tenseness is more productive of ulcer than are other varieties. Mrs. Hardy had not developed an ulcer; nor had many other of the Mrs. Hardy's whom I have seen.

Perhaps the businessman who alternates between the tensions of hope and of uncertainty gets ulcers more frequently. There are no reliable statistics on these matters. Certain psychiatrists have developed theories about the type of personality that eventuates in ulcer; but no real evidence has been presented.

The story is this. During the early nineteen-twenties, medical opinion generally attributed the origin of these ulcers to infection. Toward the end of this decade in a book called *Progressive Relaxation* addressed to doctors, I suggested that they might better look to the tense state of the individuals who developed this type of malady. As yet there was no proof. This was to a large extent furnished in later years when Lester Dragstedt and other surgeons cut the vagus nerve in cats which leads to the stomach and adjacent intestines and spurs them on to activity. Deprived of this incoming wire, this section of the digestive tract relaxed and the ulcer tended to heal and there was less recurrence. Less acid was secreted also, and the burning several hours after a big meal which marks an ulcer was lessened or disappeared.

Here was proof. However, the prior success of my suggestion often leads me to wish that matters which I have really proved would find as ready acceptance.

Be that as it may, current medical opinion generally agrees that the nervous, overzealous individual with his anxieties is a good candidate for "ulcers". Why this appears to be true can be discussed in this chapter.

In the overtense person, it would seem, the stomach churns overtime and the acidity runs high. The lining of the stomach is protected against ulcer formation by substances locally present, not wholly known as yet. When the wall becomes overtense, I venture to suggest, circulation is impaired because the blood vessels therein are squeezed unduly. But adequate circulation is necessary for the protection of any tissue; in the absence thereof, irritants tend to provoke ulcer formation. This is merely a theory; but it suggests an order of research to answer an important question.

There is another matter which calls for thought. How can we explain the association of ulcer with the presence of habitual overtenseness in daily life? Why do overtense business executives, for instance, suffer from ulcers so frequently?

According to my impression (founded on lengthy clinical experience which nevertheless falls short of proof), the stomach shares the excessive tension when we engage in undue efforts in our daily lives. My teacher, the distinguished Walter B. Cannon of Harvard, first demonstrated in cats the "spastic" state of the stomach when in the presence of dogs. Anger stopped digestion. The words "tense" and "tension" were not yet in vogue, for in the first decade of this century the scientific relaxation of these pages had not yet been developed.

Now we can say clearly that the cat which sees the dog becomes tense all over, in each and every muscle. Externally we see her back arching; her fur stands on end, her pupils enlarge, various glands pour out secretions, doubtless including epinephrine, her blood pressure rises, she becomes prepared for flight or fight. She hisses, spits and scratches.

It is no time for digestion. This is an emergency! Something must be done at once! The whole organism is called into action, just as might occur in a nation suddenly alerted for war!

It is a time for decision, as are all emergencies. Decision by an individual, whether of the cat or of the human family, depends upon how the situation faced is pictured. We might express this as follows (I do not pose as an expert in the cat language). "This dog certainly has no business on earth—not here in my presence, anyway! I might scratch his eyes out!" (Arches back, hisses, spits.) "Or perhaps it would be better to beat a safe retreat!"

If the cat has no such diction, as might be admitted freely, she nevertheless must evaluate her chances. Perhaps she "has no stomach for a fight". It is notorious that human beings may vomit before a battle.

Objectively, we know, the cat prepares externally and internally to act in the emergency. What I am here trying to add to this well-known fact is that any individual evaluates the situation which he faces, and my added theory is that the stomach walls participate in the evaluation.

Sensations from these walls certainly are present whenever I evaluate any situation or problem, for I can observe them readily. Without them, the matters with which I deal hold less interest and become devoid of color.

The sensations from the stomach walls are delicate indeed and pass unnoticed except to the highly trained observer. I have been self-trained but in earlier years have tried to pass on this type of training to university professors of psychology.

It is a fascinating field, this internal picturing which, unknown to any but the highly trained, passes our understanding and our common observation. Yet without the fine, delicate sensations which make it possible for human beings to evaluate what they experience, life would be vapid.

I have been speaking herein of an unknown world. Those who never have observed within had better skip these paragraphs, for they will mean little or nothing. As little, perhaps, as would discussions of the use of atomic energies have meant to the physicists of a bygone age!

The tenseness in our digestive tracts, then, I believe, is part and parcel of our actions and reactions to the situations and problems when we meet them with excessive effort. Externally, the tenseness can mean indigestion, tending to ulcer formation or other stomach ills. Internally there are unpleasant sensations which, like the shadows in a painting or the threatening notes in music, picture an uncertain world.

Thus unawaredly we are artists within. Sometimes in our fantasies we picture a future life with no hardships to face; angels on a cloud, we play on our little harps with eternal placidity. Then there will be no growling stomachs, no ulcers!

Meanwhile, we have practical lives to lead. In this it is best for us to picture and evaluate the unpleasant in life, the menaces and the possible alternatives. For this purpose our internal pictures (be we cat or man) need to be true rather than always pleasant. Only as angels can we afford always to picture a perfect world.

Rather, it is a hard world which we face, often dangerous, sometimes calamitous. We should know this for best conduct and for survival. In this, our digestive tract helps with its ever varying sensations of comfort and discomfort.

When there is distress or pain therefrom, it is time to take heed lest our energies be depleted by needless efforts and we develop "ulcers!"

9

INDIGESTION AND COLITIS

Tradition has it that when a man is "bilious" or his digestion upset, he looks sourly upon the world; that is, his emotional state to some extent depends upon his digestive organs. Conversely, it is well known that during a period of intense fear before a battle diarrhea is common among soldiers. When a dog sees savory food, digestive juices begin to flow in his mouth and stomach (Pavlov, 1902); but when a cat sees a strange dog, all movements in the cat's stomach and intestines cease abruptly (Cannon, 1902).

During nervous or emotional states in man various parts of his digestive tract are affected, according to evidence now to be reviewed. When food leaves the mouth, it passes through a tube of muscle which promptly contracts just above the food, thus pushing it down to the stomach. This tube is called the esophagus, and the upper portion of it can be contracted at will, as in swallowing; but it is not possible, simply by determining to perform such an act, to contract the lower portion of it. Under various conditions the muscle of the esophagus contracts unduly and more or less continuously all along its course, whereupon the passage of food is delayed. We call this phenomenon spasm, and we speak of the "spastic esophagus".

Mild spasm of this sort is likely to occur when you are overemotional or agitated. This was true of two nervous persons who helped us to study the matter in the laboratory. They learned to swallow a small deflated balloon attached to a very thin, hollow rubber tube. When the balloon had descended sufficiently in the esophagus, it was suspended there by a thread attached to a tooth. The balloon was then slightly inflated and the tube was attached to a recording system, which gave us a written record of the amount of air that passed into and out of the balloon. Under these conditions, if the patient was requested to relax all the muscles of his body as far as he could control them, air passed into the balloon, showing that the muscular walls of the esophagus relaxed also. If, on the other hand, the patient was requested to engage in some form of marked mental activity, such as doing arithmetic, as a rule air promptly left the balloon, showing increased tension in the muscular walls of the esophagus. Even a fly alighting on the nose of a subject was found by another, earlier investigator to cause increased tension.

Such evidence supports the view that in highly nervous or emotional persons we should expect some measure of spasm of the esophagus to be present frequently. This expectation has been substantially confirmed in X-ray studies which I have made in past years on more than one hundred such patients. Such a study is carried out by having the patient take a single swallow of barium paste, which is opaque to X-rays and therefore can be readily identified by the dark shadow it produces. In the normal students tested, all the paste passed through the esophagus in about one minute or less, but in nervous patients there generally is considerable delay, which in severe conditions may exceed an hour. Such delay indicates some degree of spasm.

It is well known that there are many causes of spasm of the esophagus besides nervous or emotional states. Among such causes are ulcer of the stomach, acute appendicitis and other irritating conditions. A long list of these has been compiled by a doctor interested chiefly in organic derangements. Accordingly, before we conclude that the spasm found in any individual is due merely to overactive nerves, a careful examination must be made to determine whether the patient is free from any local source of irritation, such as an inflammation or a tumor. It is important that the individual who suspects that he has spasm should consult his physician, because his discomfort may be caused by an ulcer or even by cancer.

If nervous overactivity is as widespread as many believe and if this tends to be reflected in spasm of the esophagus, we need not be surprised that, according to Dr. Clyde Brooks, spasm of the esophagus is the most common of all the ailments of the digestive tract. The symptoms vary somewhat and do not always include difficulty in swallowing to a degree noticeable by the patient. Most typically, in the moderate or incipient conditions, which predominate in number over the severe types and to which our discussion is limited, the patient mentions a "lump in the throat" or "choking sensation" or "a feeling of tightness or pressure" usually somewhere in the front portion of the chest or upper part of the abdomen, but sometimes passing to the back. At times there may be a dull ache or even intense pangs of pain. The sensation is not generally relieved, except for a brief period, by the taking of food or by alkaline powders and not altogether by moving the bowels. Belching of air may be frequent in such conditions and usually brings partial temporary relief. Sometimes the patient swallows air but does not know it and does not know how to stop it; there result distress and a feeling of fullness in the upper part of the abdomen. The distress generally does not occur at any particular period of the day; nevertheless its peculiar character and location often lead the doctor to suspect ulcer of the stomach or duodenum, and he must use great caution to avoid mistakes.

One of the persons who aided in the studies above mentioned was a nineteen-year-old university student. When first seen in January 1923 he complained of a severe cramping or burning pain in the upper part of the abdomen, which had been continuous for hours each day during the previous three years. Under the X-ray, his duodenum did not seem quite normal; there appeared to be a slight fleck or scar, as if he had once had an ulcer there. He frequently experienced a feeling of fright which he could not distinguish from the pain. This appeared particularly when he was under nervous strain, such as when he recited in class or when he was present at large gatherings or in the company of the other sex. He mentioned also frequent feelings of irritability and difficulty in concentration.

Neither our aims here nor the space available permit us to give a detailed account of the condition of this individual or of his progress as he learned to relax. This has been done sufficiently in another place (*Progressive Relaxation*, 1938). But some of the chief points in his history are interesting to recall. About three weeks after the onset of his pain, he had lost ten pounds and had become somewhat weak. A few months later he was examined by a competent internist, who, because of a certain apparent relation of the distress to meal-times, at first suspected that the patient had an ulcer of the duodenum. But after many careful examinations it was decided that probably there was no active ulcer. Accordingly, a year or so later he was sent to a neurologist, who talked to him severely and succeeded in curing him of certain fears directed toward women; but he was left with other fears and with the severe pain.

Our studies, made with the aid of the balloon as well as the X-ray methods, indicated that when he was fearful and in pain simultaneous evidences of contraction in the various muscles of his body could be readily observed. As he learned to relax these muscles, the symptoms he complained of seemed to decrease accordingly. Individual tests by the balloon and X-ray methods revealed that during a period of pain and distress, accompanied, as said above, by visible muscle tensions, the instruction to relax those tensions was followed by a prompt or gradually progressive relaxation of the esophagus, with relief from distress as long as the relaxation was maintained. The period of treatment required was unusually long, but in approximately two years, he stated that he was usually free from pain. Since then, when relapses have occurred, they have appeared to the patient as well as to the physician to be due to failure to keep up his practice and to apply what he learned. While on the whole he has made headway against his earlier habits of overactive nerves and while he has become better balanced emotionally, he has had to contend with a singularly sensitive digestive tract and some years ago suffered from a hemorrhage, presumably from the duodenum. Under these conditions it became necessary to supplement the treatment with non-irritating diet and medication. Since he complained that whenever pain recurred he noticed that he had been in a tense state previously, it seemed best to continue to coach him in advanced techniques of relaxation. In consequence he generally appeared more relaxed.

Our studies, then, support the view that the esophagus is active in emotional states and that it is part of the mechanism involved in your adjustment to your daily affairs. When you meet difficulties, and particularly if you are seldom free from them, the esophagus varies in its tensions from moment to moment, but on the whole an increase in tension is characteristic; and so we may say that the esophagus is frequently somewhat spastic. The symptoms may be slight, or they may trouble you to such an extent that you consult a doctor. The evidence suggests that the symptoms from the esophagus depend for their presence upon tensions in the outer, or skeletal, muscles and can be controlled if the individual learns to relax these muscles by the methods described in the second section of this book. It should be emphasized that a mere superficial carrying out of such directions should not be expected to effect such control if marked pain is present. In any event persons with painful conditions should be in the charge of their physician.

Much of what has been said concerning the esophagus would seem to apply also to the large intestine or colon. This organ, like the esophagus and other sections of the digestive tract, is a hollow, tubelike structure, the walls of which in a healthy person are composed mostly of muscle. Although variations in chronic overtenseness or spasticity in the esophagus doubtless are not always accompanied by similar variation in the colon, it has seemed in my experience to be generally true that the person with a more or less spastic colon has also a tendency toward spastic esophagus and vice versa. We are led to suspect that constipation, so prevalent in this country and in so many cases associated with spastic colon, is due in large measure to the overactive nervous lives we lead.

When the doctor tells you that you have "colitis" but that he has failed to find any bacteria or amoeba or any inflammation or other local irritation, he is likely to add that he believes that your bowel symptoms are due to your nervous tendencies. Perhaps there have been frequent bowel movements or diarrhea, with air passing often by rectum; or perhaps there have been thin, firm stools shaped like ribbons or like cigarettes. Inspection from time to time may disclose mucus, whereupon the condition is termed "mucous colitis". Abdominal pain in many instances is severe and cramplike before the bowels move and at other times. The distress as well as the diarrhea or constipation may become particularly marked on divers occasions such as after partaking of certain foods which seem to disagree with you or after unusual physical exertion or after contracting a cold, but they are particularly characteristic following periods of nervous and mental strain. Under the X-ray, if a meal including barium has been taken eight to twenty hours previously, the colon is seen irregularly narrowed in its various parts, sometimes almost to the point of being completely closed. In chronic cases of long standing a certain smooth and distended appearance of the colon suggests to the experienced eye that the intestinal muscle has become somewhat reduced and atrophied, presumably due to years of spasticity.

In chronic nervous colitis correct diagnosis is particularly important because of the danger of unnecessary operations. This danger arises because in this condition tenderness in the region of the appendix or gall bladder is often found and can be mistaken for inflammation requiring surgery. Rollin T. Woodyatt cited such a case, in which an operation was almost performed after a severe colonic spasm was revealed by the Roentgen ray. Fortunately, later films proved negative, and the operation was avoided. But when tenderness is found near the gall bladder or the appendix or both, as often occurs in this common malady, who can say how many futile operations are performed for this condition each year? My own experience, as previously said, suggests that there are many. Evarts Graham in his surgical address at the opening of the Medical School of the University of Chicago also warned against this error.

An interesting illustration may be briefly recounted. Mrs. E. T., fifty-eight years old, a member of a notable Irish family, complained in January 1922 that for the past thirty years she had been subject to attacks of mucous colitis. They had increased in frequency until now they had appeared two or three times a month. They were increasing in severity also, for pain had been marked during the last four years all over the abdomen, sometimes shooting down the thighs, sometimes passing with a burning sensation up under the sternum. These attacks generally lasted for about two days, and the pain could be relieved only by an electric pad and by a dose of baking soda. Cramping abdominal pain occurred with any bowel movement, and distress in the upper part of the abdomen appeared usually within five to ten minutes after eating or drinking. This pain generally disappeared spontaneously an hour or two after eating. At times she was constipated and often weak, she said, and unable to engage in normal activities.

The examining hand found the colon firm along its entire course and tender particularly near the regions of the gall bladder and the appendix. In the X-ray film a highly spastic colon was revealed, so narrowed near the spleen that it appeared like a stricture. This was no cancer, for the colon filled out when an enema containing barium was given. Although previous treatment through restriction of diet and the use of various medicines had failed to effect lasting improvement, for several months I also attempted to relieve the condition through these measures. I had not previously applied progressive relaxation to chronic colitis, and, oddly enough, in this case it was the consulting surgeon who suggested that progressive relaxation be tried.

Treatment by progressive relaxation was accordingly begun in May. The study was of additional interest because other measures, including diet and rest, had been carefully employed without satisfactory effect. This patient was not very apt at learning to recognize muscular contractions. Among the striking tensions outwardly revealed was a persistent severe frown and a frequently wrinkled forehead. Much practice was devoted to relaxing these regions. During the months as she became relaxed in these and other parts, the hospital records showed a gradual disappearance of mucus from the stools. By August, when the patient was still in the hospital, the gall-bladder region had become entirely free from tenderness, and pain had become diminished or absent. The stools as a rule had become normal.

At home the patient continued without further medical aid to improve at relaxing her muscles, just as an individual will improve with practice after instruction in piano playing or dancing or other physical skills. After about six months more the tenderness had disappeared from the abdomen completely. She went to California, nursed her husband, who had become ill, swam and drove a motorcar with impunity for the first time in many years. An X-ray film kindly made for me at LaJolla three years after the beginning of treatment revealed a colon no longer extremely spastic. Colonic pain was absent excepting after housework, which she therefore avoided. Two years after the X-ray she stated that her general condition had been highly satisfactory for five years with only slight relapses. She continued to practice relaxation regularly, particularly if she felt any difficulties coming on.

When last I saw her, frowning seemed very greatly diminished. She had had no recurrences, was on full diet and appeared very well.

Striking as are these results, six months of treatment is considered insufficient to eradicate habitual colonic spasm in patients so ill. As education in the field of relaxation progresses, it is to be hoped that people will seek more than increased comfort and the abatement of symptoms. Maladies entrenched for years in unhealthful nervous habits should be treated thoroughly by these newer methods until results are attained securely, as judged by objective standards.

Patients differ greatly in the degree of skill they acquire in continuing habits of relaxation they have learned. Some, neglecting practice, tend to retrogress, but even with these I am inclined to believe that relaxation once well learned is, like swimming, more or less a permanent possession. I have seen instances where, in spite of reported faithful practice, retrogression has occurred, at least for a time; but the rule, on the whole, has seemed to be in the direction of the adage that practice makes perfect.

Of late years more than thirty cases of marked spastic or mucous colitis have been treated by relaxation alone, with the patient on full diet practically from the outset; and if we consider only those cases in which treatment and practice were regularly maintained for a year or more as directed by the physician, the results have been in most cases a gradual abatement of symptoms and resumption of normal vigor.

In addition to actual colitis, we should mention the spells of abdominal symptoms frequent in many nervous persons, which are like those seen in outright cases of spastic colitis except that they are not so severe; the course of these evidently could be controlled by the introduction of relaxation and recurrence probably prevented.

In 1929 experience in the treatment of ulcer of

the stomach and duodenum prompted me to suggest that these maladies might be of nervous origin and that physicians might very well investigate whether they would not subside in patients trained to relax. Careful investigation was extremely difficult because of the frequent necessity of medication and diet. Prior to this suggestion, it had been generally believed that infection played a primary role in the causation of such ulcers. However, following my suggestion, the view became widely prevalent among physicians that peptic ulcer arises in nervous people. While impressed with the agreement of clinicians on this point, I admitted in earlier editions of this volume that scientific investigations remained to be made.

In résumé, I have proved, at least in the several persons studied, that during marked emotion various parts of the digestive tract take part, becoming increasingly tense or spastic. If nerves are chronically overactive, various symptoms may arise from the parts of the digestive tract most affected. In these conditions tenderness in particular regions should not be mistaken for severe inflammation requiring surgery. The evidence to date indicates that the common cases of spastic portions of the digestive tract may be favorably treated through relaxation.

In chronic colitis and in peptic ulcer, if your doctor has advised relaxation:

Practice lying down at least one half hour before each meal.

Watch for frowning or other habitual tensions and eliminate these.

Be sure to learn to relax your abdominal muscles.

Make differential relaxation a habit during your daily affairs.

Chew food slowly, masticate well, use smaller and less frequent swallows.

10

COMMON NERVOUS AND MENTAL DISORDERS

"Nervousness" varies from time to time and from person to person like the waves of the ocean. But forms can be distinguished, and to these are given special names.

"High nerve tension" or "overactive nerves" are terms that seem to cover the forms which we meet most commonly. If you inquire and observe among your neighbors, you may be amazed to see how common nervous characteristics are—how seldom you find families free from them.

One person fails to sleep well; another (or the same one) is frequently overfatigued; a third worries almost incessantly; a fourth avoids long drives for fear of accidents; a fifth is unable to sit through a motion picture or the opera; a sixth is too restless to read and study as he formerly did; a seventh (and there are many sevenths!) is irritated and quarrelsome at home; an eighth is oppressed by his business duties and so on.

In all of these persons, as previously said, you can with care observe outward signs of excess tension—now in this muscle group, now in that. This excess tension obviously increases when the nervous symptoms become acute and commonly disappears when they subside.

In some of the foregoing examples one symptom or group of symptoms stands out. Perhaps it is nervousness during speaking: the individual stammers or stutters. If you inquire in detail, you find that the difficulties of each sufferer are somewhat specialized; each becomes particularly nervous or tense in saying—or in imagining that he is saying—certain sounds or in speaking to certain persons or in meeting particular types of situations.

Perhaps the outstanding symptom is fear, either reasonable or unwarranted.

Herbert Spencer maintained that without fear man could never have advanced beyond primitive states. Anticipation of future difficulties—however disagreeable—prepares the way to meet them with success. Thus fear is the great saver from harm, the great educator.

At a moment of marked fear, if our electrical recording instrument is suitably attached, currents are found to run high and frequent in almost any nerve or muscle. This is what we have called nervousness. If Spencer was right, nervousness at times can be very useful.

However, as any reader has witnessed, fears may become prolonged and excessive. Then they constitute a burden on the nervous system and may lead toward disorders in other systems as well. There comes a stage in certain cases where it becomes difficult to say whether the fear is merely an exaggerated normal state or a somewhat pathological one. But if the individual fears that he will jump out of a window when in high buildings or that he may stab somebody if a knife lies about, we call the fear definitely pathological and label it a *phobia*.

It is not considered sufficient in treating such a condition through relaxation for the patient to learn to be relaxed merely when lying down. Rather, it seems necessary for the patient to learn to recognize when and where he is tense during the experience of fear and to relax the localities involved. This is differential relaxation.

"Worry" is the complaint perhaps most often heard by the doctor in the field of nervous medicine. Can modern science contribute anything toward the solution of the problem of worry? In the past, most laymen and many doctors have been inclined to believe that the only way to remedy worry is to "remove the cause" and that the cause of worry lies solely in the difficulties which we meet in life. But what really *is* the cause? Is it solely in those difficulties, or is it also in ourselves? Doubtless the quickest way to effect a cure of a particular worry is to remedy the matter of concern—for example, to provide funds for those who worry about poverty. But too often such provision is not feasible. Furthermore, certain losses cannot be remedied at all—for example, the death of a loved one. And in every life, trying situations inevitably arise from time to time. We are faced with the fact that practically the same kind of dangers and losses will lead one person to extreme worry and irritability but leave another relatively calm and self-possessed.

Granted that worry is a subjective state which is incited but not wholly caused by various matters which arise in the lives of everyone, what can be done about it? In many, worrying becomes a habit; reassurance and argument commonly seem of little avail; the more the talk, the more, at least in some cases, does the worry seem to recur. Most persons tend to review the troublesome matter again and again in an effort to find a solution, even if only the imaginative one, "It might have been different!" To escape such thoughts, resort often is made to change of scene, to distracting occupation, to exercise and baths, perchance to drink or to sedative drugs; but most commonly the problems of the worrisome individual are not solved. If fortune favors or if time heals the wound, a new source of distress soon appears on the horizon—to be followed by another and another. The worrying tendency persists and ever finds something new to feed upon.

The physician of today must prepare himself to deal with the problem of worry. *Many persons successfully engaged in useful occupations find themselves in need of treatment.* It is extremely doubtful that methods of reassuring or of distracting them are sufficiently effective.

In training nervous persons to relax, the patients are directed, as previously indicated, in methods of observing what they do subjectively when they worry. They note tensions of which, as they assert, they have been previously unconscious. As illustrated above, many patients, previously trained to observe, report that when they engage in worry, they picture something—however vaguely and briefly—connected with the matter of worry and at that moment have tensions as in looking at what they have pictured; or they say something about it to themselves or to others and at that moment have tensions in the speech muscles. So, if they have lost money, they may for a time tend to review pictorially the events connected with their making the investment and an observer may possibly note eye movements and persistent frowning.

Treatment is to be directed toward the voluntary but also the habitual relaxation of tensions specifically accompanying the worrying. That is, if you are such a worrier, you are to learn to relax the eyes so as not to review visual impressions of

the events connected with your making the investment. There is much clinical evidence that this
can be done to an adequate extent without your
closing your eyes, even while you continue to
engage in daily affairs. When instructed to relax
such tensions, trained observers report that the
process of worry ceases for the moment at least.
Such reports are secured even when the physician
takes every precaution to avoid hinting that a
therapeutic effect will be accomplished. In many
instances, in fact, patients apparently do not understand clearly what the method is all about until
the cessation of worry dawns upon them at least
partially a *fait accompli.*

Observation on worried patients suggests that
their moments of concern involve particularly
often the knitting of the brows, although this
tension occurs commonly in most persons when
they are thinking actively or facing relatively
bright light. It may be of interest for you to note
how often this tension occurs in persons you meet.
Darwin considered tension in this region significant, noting that the animal which frowns or
contracts his brows is meeting difficulty. Under
this assumption, if a worrisome patient reports or
seems to show such tension more or less habitually, he is drilled particularly in relaxing this region.
If you are such a person, you are to practice
relaxing the brow, as instructed in Chapters 13
and 14. These methods obviously apply no less if
worry occurs to a pathological extent.

We are sometimes told that the only way to find out why a person is melancholic or has certain fears, habits of worry or other emotional symptoms is to search his past for psychic causes. Such assumptions are not part of the approach described in this volume. Rather our method is to observe what the patient is doing muscularly at the moment when his melancholy, fear, worry or other mental symptoms are present, and if we can identify particular patterns of contraction, however slight, we proceed as best we can to eliminate them. If successful in this elimination, as judged by objective standards, we find that the symptoms tend to disappear.

If you are a worrier or are slightly inclined to "the blues", there probably are many issues which concern you needlessly, perhaps producing sleeplessness for many hours into the night. It may seem to you that you must find the answer to some problem in hand or that somehow you must overcome a certain source of irritation. Perhaps the issue is:

"To be or not to be—
That is the question!"

The best way that I know to handle morbid states of worry is to *keep in mind the distinction between the issue and the attitude.* You must observe that at such moments your attitude is overtense. If you relax the excess tension present in various muscle groups, you attain a quietude of demeanor, and you are likely to report a lessened interest in the issue. Questions that seemed fundamental, crying for an answer, may still appeal to your intellect but no longer affect your emotions so intensely. With habits of advancing relaxation, you tend to become able to adjust yourself to the living conditions you meet, perhaps not approving those conditions but nevertheless not permitting them to render you overemotional and unfit. I find, however, that the learner needs to be reminded over and over again, when he becomes engrossed in a troublesome matter, to distinguish between the issue and the attitude.

Enough has been said to illustrate the importance of teaching nervous and neurotic patients to observe their tensions and to relax and of checking their continual success by recorded action-potential measurements. These methods can be applied not only to conditions previously mentioned in this chapter but also to other forms of mental disorder, including undue exaltation and depression.

On the side of treatment, the results already secured in various disorders by progressive relaxation seem to warrant wide usage of the method. Except in acute cases of nervousness, the results are obtained slowly and are therefore not spectacular. But since they depend upon habits gradually and firmly acquired by the patient, it is not surprising that the improvement attained should have notably endured over a term of years. Most of what has been said in the present chapter arises from observations and interpretations in clinical practice. This is suggestive and important but not yet a science; laboratory investigations are being conducted on an extensive scale. Available methods now supply objective indications of the patient's progress, since objective confirmation is better than mere opinion of the patient or physician.

11

HOW TO SLEEP WELL

Various factors can "stir up" the nerves and muscles leading away from the restful sleep which conserves our personal energy, adenosine triphosphate. Aside from the overstimulation of modern living, yet interwoven therewith, are cares and anxieties and sometimes "pangs of conscience". Shakespeare has made us familiar with these in his "uneasy lies the head that wears a crown" and "Macbeth hath murdered sleep".

Less dramatically, we list coffee and tea in persons sensitive to caffeine. Hunger pangs are not conducive to sleep. This tendency is useful, for the pangs lead the hungry animal to seek food before he becomes too weak. However, unless severe, the pangs may disappear for the time being if the individual rests successfully.

Many persons complain that they cannot sleep when it is too hot or when the atmosphere is stuffy. Residents in torrid climes, however, generally succeed in sleeping each night, while many animals seek caves as a favorite place for rest, regardless of fresh air. Evidently the complainers mentioned do not know how to adapt themselves to their environment. Noises are the bane of the existence of many poor sleepers. In consequence, they often insist on extremely quiet locations for their beds and go to various extremes to avoid disturbance. Their very efforts to improve their state, as we shall see later, create a vicious circle, resulting in insomnia. Similar results are seen in those who wear dark cloths to cover the eyes during rest.

It is certain that sleep is a habit very easily disturbed in those who are given to much intellectual work or reflection. Whatever interrupts sleep one night may lead to a period of awakening on the following night, often approximately at the same time.

Exercise in moderation promotes sleep in a healthy manner, because fatigue products are formed, which lead to the natural consequence. Possibly for invalids massage may act as a substitute. Other measures, such as the taking of warm milk regardless of appetite, prolonged immersion in a warm bath or the use of alcoholic beverages, may promote the onset of sleep on a particular occasion in some individuals, but they are approaches to the problem of insomnia from the wrong angle.

In a book on sleep by the present author, an imaginary doctor, described by the critics as a "fussy, fictional character", is asked by his patient, "What prevents sleep?"

"What prevents sleep?" he repeats impressively. "The answer is very simple", with a sidelong glance and, pointing with the stem of his pipe, "You!"

"There you are, lying on your bed at night, fidgeting and fuming and fretting that you can't go to sleep. Doubled-up postures, holding down the bed, disordered bedclothes! Why can't you sleep? Precisely because you fidget and fume and fret, either about your loss of sleep or about some other matters, most often some trouble, real or imaginary. It becomes a vicious circle: your fidgets turn aside sleep and your insomnia leads to more fidgets until the more you think about your insomnia and your other troubles, the more you lose sleep. What is the answer? That's what I'm going to try to tell you. But first I want you to understand more fully just why you lose sleep.

"You say that you *can't* sleep; you believe that you *can't* sleep. But can you prove it? Not at all! The most you can prove is that until a certain moment on any night, you did not fall asleep. In spite of repeated attempts, you failed. What do you mean by 'can't'? If you push against a brick wall with all your weight, you are right in saying,

'I can't push it down'. Your proof would be that the wall is solid and heavy, out of all proportion to your strength; but in the same sense you would not be able to prove that you could not sleep. If these newer views are correct, the reason that you fail to sleep is because some of your muscles are tense when they should not be; and who is responsible for this tensing? Your grandmother, whose features you inherit? Your boss, because he scolded you this morning? No! *You* are responsible! *You* are the person doing it!

"Perhaps you feel like saying that when you are tense, you just can't help it. That is what is called a 'good alibi'! If you want to continue to be tense and need an excuse to do so, all I can say is that *your excuses are excellent.*

"Instead of making excuses, consider the facts. There you lie, failing to sleep, because you are repeatedly shifting or moving about in order to become more comfortable. It is certain that, if your nerves and muscles are intact, when you move an arm in order to change something in bed, you have the ability *not to do it.* I do not mean that you should restrain yourself from doing it, for this commonly means that you hold yourself quiet, which is being tense, not relaxed. I mean that if you have the ability to bend your arm, you normally have the ability not to. *Ipso facto,* as the lawyers say. The fact is that when you move about in bed, seeking comfort, it is you doing so; nothing compels you. You are led to do it by your own desires and habits; that is all.

"Your mistake is that you are ever trying to become a little more comfortable or to avoid discomfort."

"That is natural", you reply.

"But I am reminded of the lesson of Jesus—the paradox that only by sacrificing your life can you save it. Only by sacrificing your comfort at the moment, when you lie awake—relaxing in the face of discomfort—can you eventually become comfortable and go to sleep. It is your persistent effort to better yourself that results in failure; your effort is tension.

"You are much the same in your daily living. All day long you are on a tension to meet your appointments, to make a good impression or to convince your customers. This is your effort to better your state, to make yourself more comfortable in life. You have the habit of being tense in one or another set of muscles or nerves all day long, as part of your life plan for accomplishment. You fail to relax for even one moment of the day. I say to you that you would stand a better chance to accomplish all your purposes and with greater ease if you would leave out some of this continual straining. Learn to be a little more relaxed, instead!"

If what has previously been said is true, the basis for insomnia inevitably has been laid in our habits of overtense living. When a physical object goes very fast, we say that it has momentum, and if the object is heavy we do not expect a mere touch to slow it down. In the same way, when a human being habitually speeds the responses of very many different nerves and muscles and keeps up this rate with only occasional moderate remissions hour after hour during the day, we should naturally expect something of this speed to continue in his tissues long into the night.

The question of how to shut off your energies at night had been largely neglected when, in 1908, I turned to the subject of relaxation, including sleep. The textbook in physiology then and until recently more in vogue in certain medical schools taught that little was known about sleep and advocated the theory that it depended upon conditions of blood pressure.

This and certain other views on sleep current at that time did not seem supported by the results of my early studies. In 1910 in Ithaca I was testing how strong odor sensations appear to subjects under certain conditions. Upon carefully watching the subjects while they paid attention to the source of smell, I found that they engaged in certain tensions. Obviously, various muscles were contracting as they leaned forward, looked at the source of odor, frowned, wrinkled their foreheads, breathed in the odors jerkily and often spoke unnecessarily. Accordingly, without telling them why, I requested them to "abandon all effort" and I instructed them somewhat in relaxing the observed tensions, so that they might smell and pass judgment with a minimum of exertion. Under these conditions, the subjects evidently at times were on the verge of sleep. One subject repeatedly fell asleep whenever he became sufficiently relaxed. It was a pretty clear demonstration that when a person relaxes far enough, sleep automatically ensues.[1]

A certain personal experience in 1908 also gave opportunity for observation. At that time, like many other students who always carry their work with them, I had a nightly insomnia which persisted for hours. Mental activity continued regardless of the need of rest. Upon seeking to discover what it was physiologically that seemed to keep me awake, I found that I could always identify what felt like muscular tensions somewhere in the body and that when these were eliminated by relaxation, sleep took place. Their elimination was not always a rapid process, particularly at first. But as I studied the muscle tensions further, I noted that subjectively I seemed responsible for them and therefore apparently could undo them. This evidently depended upon my carrying relaxation sufficiently far. These personal experiences, while having in no sense the character of scientific evidence, have proved of service in the selection of experiments and in the training of subjects and patients.

As far back as 1887 W. P. Lombard tapped the tendon under the kneecap and noted that the kick

[1]This study was published in 1911 from the Psychological Laboratory at Cornell University.

is decreased during sleep. Some later investigators observed no kick at all during sleep, while others, including W. W. Tuttle, found none during deep sleep, but registered slight kicks during light sleep. Our own results agree with those of Tuttle. If sleep is deep, the knee jerk, like certain other deep reflexes, cannot be aroused, but if it is light and restless the kick or other reflex response may be more or less vigorous. Accordingly, since Professor Anton J. Carlson and I found the knee-jerk greatly diminished or absent in subjects relaxed to the greatest possible extent, although still awake, we concluded that by voluntary relaxation while still awake one may attain a degree of nerve-muscle tension lower than that of light sleep.

That sleep involves general muscular relaxation was clearly stated in 1913 by Henri Piéron, a noted French investigator. He believed, however, that a person does not fall asleep because of relaxation but because of a certain chemical substance appearing in the blood following bodily activities, especially fatigue. My own observations had previously brought out the importance of relaxation in the onset and maintenance of sleep. In 1918 and subsequent years I often observed patients under treatment (or subjects during experiments) falling asleep as they became relaxed.

These individuals were trained to observe sensations from muscle tensions as described in Chapter 17. Such sensations are sometimes called "proprioceptive sensations"—although this term includes also the sensations from the skin, tendons, internal organs and other parts, which indicate to you the states of your body. I found that proprioceptive sensations are characteristic of wakefulness and that when they are diminished during progressive or sudden relaxation, sleep sets in. We do not know, in fact, that sensations from active muscles interfere more with the onset of sleep than do other sensations, such as those from touch and pressure of bedclothes, for these also are increased during muscular contractions, owing to movements of the skin and perhaps to other factors.

During more recent years my doctrine that the onset and maintenance of sleep depend particularly on the reduction of proprioceptive sensations interested other investigators. Apart from doctrine, the facts seem to be that as relaxation advances, sensory as well as motor nerve impulses diminish and that at some point sleep sets in.

That this does not necessarily depend upon fatigue has been frequently illustrated in my various studies. (We have been handicapped in attempting to make statements about fatigue because until recently we have had no convenient objective measure of it.) Patients being trained to relax for neurotic conditions other than sleeplessness, who therefore have received no suggestions concerning sleep, have usually fallen asleep during periods of general relaxation, regardless of the presence or absence of fatigue. Frequently such occurrences have been noted while the subject was connected with the electrical recording apparatus.

Here is an illustration of the connection between relaxation and sleep. A trained subject lies on a couch. His blood pressure is being taken at frequent intervals from his left arm, while his right arm is connected to wires leading to the recording system. For ten minutes during this experiment he is requested to clench his right fist continuously. That he is doing so can be readily confirmed upon watching the needle of the recording instrument dial, which vibrates violently as long as the fist is being clenched. But in spite of the instruction, moments occur when fairly suddenly the needle becomes quiet, showing that the subject quickly relaxes the muscles of his hand; at such moments he snores. Again, if the operator suddenly hears snoring as he looks at the needle on the dial screen, he sees the needle become quiet. Thereupon, when the operator tells the subject to resume clenching his fist the needle again vibrates, and the snoring ceases. Although we thus have a means of determining precisely the instant when the subject becomes completely relaxed, we have no such means of determining the precise onset of sleep, because the signs of sleep do not distinguish it sharply from general relaxation.

The onset of sleep, then, can be very abrupt.

It is commonly effected, according to my clinical observations, at the moment when the eyes and the speech apparatus relax (approximately) completely. The complete relaxation in these particular parts need not be prolonged, I believe, for more than a brief interval; my conjecture is for not more than half a minute. When some subjects fall asleep, the recording needle continues to show relaxation. In others, after an interval of quiet, it soon shows series of marked vibrations. If at such an instant the subject is awakened by the operator, he reports having been dreaming.

Our findings, then, suggest the correctness of the view that the deepest sleep (the most relaxed sleep) is free or relatively free from dreaming.

Restless sleep is generally considered to be not so refreshing as sleep free from frequent movements. Fifteen thousand measurements were taken on eleven subjects lying in beds, wherein certain movements could be recorded. The investigator, Dr. H. M. Johnson, found that during eight hours' sleep at night the average period free from such recorded movements was but eleven and one-half minutes. Such results, however, do not mean that his subjects were relaxed during the intervals between the movements recorded; for his apparatus was not sufficiently sensitive to measure the slighter forms of muscular rigidity and motion.

According to the same psychologist, healthy sleepers shift from one gross bodily position to another between twenty and forty-five times in the course of a typical night of eight hours. Each of these stirs is separated from its nearest neighbor by at least two and a half minutes. He concluded that such "sleep motility" is normal and serves a useful purpose. His conclusion that moving about is desirable in sleep runs counter to common experience. While shifting may satisfy a need of the moment, I have found every indication and suggestion that the quieter the sleeper, the better his rest. Individuals trained to relax can be observed or measured during restful sleep, revealing that movements of the type observed by Johnson are infrequent or altogether absent over extended periods of time.

While sleep can be discussed in terms of relaxation, there are various measures to bring on this state aside from those discussed previously. No more brilliant example can be cited than one shown in the moving-picture demonstration before a world congress of physiologists in Boston in the early thirties. Professor L. Hess, a Swiss scientist, showed a number of cats which had undergone operations in which he had inserted and securely fastened fine wires leading through the skull to certain tiny regions in the brain: the gray matter near the intermediate mass and near the head end of the aqueduct which connects the brain cavities. Following the operations the cats had recovered fully and seemed normal in every way. When he connected the wires protruding from the skull with a source of faint electric current, he could stimulate the particular regions mentioned. Thereupon each cat would quickly find itself a comfortable place and go off to sleep. If he stimulated these regions with a strong current, the cat, while in the act of walking off somewhere, would appear to be suddenly deterred from further action, often falling down at once, as if literally thrown into sleep.

When you see or hear or have other sensations, Hess concluded, you are kept awake; but in his experiments and in various ways under normal conditions, the lines leading up to the brain can be interrupted, whereupon incoming messages dwindle or cease, and so you sleep.

In 1930 at the University of Chicago, desiring to study eye movements during visualization in waking states and during dreams, I solved the problem electronically by developing what in recent decades has been known as electrooculography (EOG).

My EOG methods of recording eye movements during waking and dream states were applied in my own but not in other laboratories until the late nineteen-fifties. Then after N. Kleitman had read about my recordings and had visited my laboratory, he sent his graduate student, E. Azerinsky, to consult me in order to learn how to record eye movements during dreams. After learning how, they applied my electronic EOG techniques to dreams as I had done. They noted what they designated as "REM", rapid eye movements marking dream visualization. Subsequently scores of studies and articles thereon followed by other writers, blissfully ignorant of the early history of EOG development and its application to dreams. Incidentally, writers of these articles on REM generally do not even mention the application of progressive relaxation to sound sleep and the possible lessening of dream states, which is one of the chief subjects of the present chapter.

In severe fatigue the level of tension present when sleep begins evidently can be very high; for in this way we can explain how soldiers on the march, nearing exhaustion, may go to sleep yet continue walking. The monotony of the march apparently favors this phenomenon. Many persons have fallen asleep while driving a car over long stretches. I have done so more than once on a clear country road at night, notwithstanding the tensions in my leg engaged with the accelerator pedal, those in my arms engaged with steering and those in my neck upholding my head. This illustrates that sleep can come on even in the presence of a certain degree and spread of tension, but such tension must be relatively unvarying, and there must be monotony. What prevents slumber and keeps us awake is quick changes; we can go to sleep (if fatigue products are sufficient) even under conditions of tension, provided that there is no sudden variation, arising from stimuli either outside or inside us, including our own muscles.[2]

Accordingly, you can fall asleep (1) if sufficiently relaxed or (2) even if tense in certain respects, provided that the tensions are maintained steadily. Sleep commencing under tension, as noted, is generally marked by observable movements and fidgets of the sleeper and by dreams; the sleeper also reports later that the sleep has not been completely restful. In "tense" sleep (so to call it) a freely hanging leg kicks vigorously when tapped with a hammer on the tendon below the patella, but in relaxed sleep the kick is slighter or absent altogether. As you fall asleep, if you have been tense in the preceding hours you may jump or jerk all over your body or in some part of it. This is the sleep start. You should ignore it and relax again to sleep; evidently you have been relaxing well just before it occurred, though poorly during the preceding minutes or hours. Accordingly, the sleep start does not occur at night if you have been fairly relaxed during the previous hours of the day.

In clinical experience, restless sleep follows a variety of conditions, such as continual mental activity during the day, particularly if this involved effort or excitement and if it was prolonged up to the moment of retiring; various sorts of

[2]Apparently the onset of sleep depends upon monotony—that is, the first derivative of tension.

emotional excitement, pleasant or unpleasant; overfatigue; fever; the presence of pain or other distress, including excessive warmth or cold; unaccustomed sudden or intermittent sensory disturbances, such as noises; coffee and certain other stimulants. Relaxed sleep is favored by whatever factors tend to promote differential relaxation during the day's activities as well as by a moderate amount of exercise.

The nervous patient often seems to be hard to satisfy in his sleeping environment. He makes many adjustments. Upon lying down he shifts this way and that, seeking comfort and perhaps finding it, but generally not for long. Many a sleepless person, I have observed, changes his position every few minutes for hours, but the repeated movements cause continued insomnia. Individuals of this type commonly live their daily lives in a similar manner, seldom quite content with what they have or meet with, ever striving for some end not quite attained and keeping active by day as well as by night (at least in thought) to achieve it. To overcome such tendencies insofar as they hamper sleep it is necessary for the individual to realize that he is not to wait to relax until he first has become comfortable but rather is to take any position that seems fairly comfortable and then to relax in that position in spite of any subsequent discomfort.

In treatment by relaxation no additional means are used to induce sleep; otherwise, when sleep is achieved, we cannot be certain what has been responsible. Furthermore, it seems better to learn to avoid external aids, in the interest of self-dependence. Those who have become dependent on sedative drugs take longer to learn to relax in natural sleep.

Many years ago doctors awoke to the realization that they had frequently treated chronic constipation by means of cathartics and enemas in vain; indeed in many patients such practices can be actually held responsible for the development of chronic constipation. This is known as the "cathartic habit". Similarly, chronic insomnia can result from taking sedatives habitually. How this comes about is illustrated by a patient under treatment. As a test to see whether it would reduce her blood pressure, she was given a sizable dose (three grains) of sodium amytal three times a day, but she was kept in ignorance of the kind of medicine. Although her pressure was not reduced even after eight days of medication, she complained that she was so sleepy that she rode by her station when on the car and was generally inefficient. A week after she had ceased to take the sedative, she volunteered the information that, strange as it might seem, she no longer was able to fall asleep by day (when she rested) as she had prior to the medication. Here was an instance of insomnia in the making! *The individual who becomes accustomed to aids in relaxation in the form of sedatives becomes less able to relax spontaneously.*

Patients who come to the physician can be

separated into two classes: those who have been sleeping little or restlessly for a relatively short period such as a few days or weeks or even months, and those who have so suffered for years. In medical practice the methods of relaxation, in a highly abbreviated form, can be useful in showing an ill person how to rest more quietly at once, but the results may not be lasting unless treatment is continued.

In general, insomnia which has been present for only a brief period will be more likely to yield quickly, other things fairly equal, than insomnia which has existed for many years. Individuals with severe chronic conditions, always associated with other symptoms of high nerve tension, are often unreasonable in their hopes of effecting a cure very promptly. They fail to understand that what they most require is a prolonged course in nervous reeducation. They do not recall that in learning any new skill, such as playing the piano or speaking a foreign language, excellence is not expected within a few weeks or months. While individuals vary greatly in the speed with which they learn to relax, a disordered condition such as insomnia which has lasted for many years commonly does not yield to treatment in less than one year and frequently requires a considerably longer time. The patient generally notes some improvement during the first month or two, but in the usual case upsetting circumstances occur from time to time, and prolonged treatment is required to render him more nearly free from relapses.

Program for Sleep

If you have been sleepless and desire to learn to shut off your energies at night through relaxation:

Cultivate habits of relaxation at night and during daily activities as directed in Chapters 13 and 14.

Remember that a tense day is likely to be followed by a tense night.

Practice lying down for an hour near noon and near sundown.

Discontinue sedative medicines gradually as soon as your doctor permits.

Assume a fairly comfortable position, and if discomfort sets in do not shift repeatedly but relax in spite of discomfort.

Remember to keep up your daily drill, or you may lose what gains you have made.

Do not be discouraged by relapses.

Above all, try to develop a complete let-go of the muscles of eyes and speech.

Learn to relax to some extent even in the presence of noises or other disturbances, including moderate distress and pain.

If you have long-standing insomnia, this book may aid appreciably, but you probably need personal instruction by a physician to acquire habits of relaxation.

12

MORE ABOUT
TENSE PERSONS

In the rush of the present day, man has in part forgotten how to live. Joy in sunlight, birds and flowers is left chiefly to the poet; delight in line and curve is sought in the studio; while interest in circumstance becomes the special task of the dramatist. This deficiency in modern living seems at least partly due to the fact that the appreciation of beauty as well as doing things beautifully demands a certain abandon. Lacking this, it would seem, many persons, defeated in the purposes of their special pursuits, become discontented—even to the point of suicide.

Modern living often is found wanting not merely artistically but also economically. In its broadest sense, economy pertains to whatever is of value. To count costs chiefly in terms of dollars is a form of materialism dominant in many parts of Western civilization. Few persons care how much they spend in terms of nervous and mental energy. When healthy they are likely to take their daily pursuits with a seriousness and intentness that would be warranted only if they were immortal. Evidently, a saner grasp on reality occurs when it is recognized that energies commonly wasted might, with the same accomplishment, be saved.

During rush and other activities involving a considerable expenditure of energy, any individual, as can readily be observed, shows signs that he is markedly contracting muscles in various parts of his body. We say that he is tense. Among your friends you can no doubt recognize some who are tense too much of the time. I should like to introduce several interesting examples as met by the physician.

First is a friendly sort of man—evidently alert, energetic and intellectual. He seems to be about thirty-seven years old and is married but childless. He is a professor and is known as a hard worker. As he chats, you note that he wrinkles his forehead often and that he holds his eyes wide open. Watching carefully, you see that he shifts some part of his body from time to time, evidently in order to make it more comfortable. Aside from these inconspicuous signs, he does not impress you as an example of a tense person until you hear his account of himself. When a student at college, he relates, he was under severe mental strain. He found himself continually thinking about his work day and night. Never a sound sleeper, he then, for the first time, began to pass many sleepless hours during the night. Particularly during the last decade, he has felt tense and has not rested well. A medical examination has failed to disclose any serious abnormality. Nevertheless he mentions a certain lassitude—a fatigue, which he states has detracted from his mental efficiency.

Another illustration is a lovely lady of about forty. She is well-to-do, manages her household and four children and still finds time to meet her social acquaintances, to serve on committees and to keep her figure lithe and agile through ballet practice. She meets this continual run of duties with outward poise, except that she is occasionally cross with the children. But she admits that she frequently feels excited and irritable and that she is full of fear when she addresses a gathering or undertakes social responsibilities. Of late she has not slept very well and at times has had nausea with frontal headaches. Like the gentleman depicted above, she has no disease that need worry her, no disorder except, obviously, her nervous and mental habits. You notice that she speaks somewhat fast and a little too much. She looks at you with eyes fairly wide open, and her expression changes frequently, as she frowns or wrinkles her forehead. Occasionally she shifts her limbs or sighs. On the whole, however, she sits fairly quietly, and it is the recital of her experiences rather than her behavior that first brings to your notice that she, also, is a tense person.

Here is a tall, well-built man, about forty-eight years old. He has the keen eye of the business executive who sizes you up at a glance. His voice is quiet and controlled, and you look in vain for outward evidences of restlessness or fidgets. However, there is something about him that makes you feel that he is tense, overalert, "just waiting to go". Like his competitors, at the present time of intense activity, he has business worries; in fact, he finds himself unable to cease thinking about his affairs. But he had similar difficulties during easier times and has often wished that he could master his business in the sense of letting it take its course rather than being continually concerned about it. An examination discloses no disease of heart, kidneys or thyroid gland. When you learn that he does not sleep well, frequently has one or more loose bowel movements per day and that his blood pressure has been high, you wonder whether these symptoms are not in some way connected with his mental characteristics.

A young lady of twenty-five shows signs which will not be hard to read. She is a stenographer, and if you watch her at work you note that she holds her back and neck somewhat stiffly. At times she almost wriggles, as if to get herself into a more comfortable position, while she frowns, wrinkles her forehead or sighs as if worried or distressed. She scarcely sits still for as long as a minute, always finding occasion to move some part of her body, such as hand or a leg. You do not feel at rest while speaking with her. You are not surprised to hear her say that she is nervous and chronically fatigued, because evidently there is no minute of the day when she is even partially at rest. Doubtless she has always been inclined to be nervous; for instance, she recalls that once, after a cyclone had been predicted, she awakened during a strong wind to find herself trembling all over. During the same year, while on a voyage to Europe, a similar trembling spell set in, this time without apparent reason. Since then she has had such spells at irregular intervals. However, her life was relatively uneventful until two years ago, when she nursed her father, who was dying of heart disease. A year later an insurance examiner informed her that she had heart leakage. This continued to worry her greatly, until she developed a feeling of terror, which was not assuaged when specialists informed her last fall that her heart was quite normal. Following this spell of fright about her own condition, she had various pains, which made her all the more fearful. Her appearance no less than her recital leaves the careful observer in no doubt that she has been in a state of high tension.

I might continue indefinitely to introduce further instances and varieties of symptoms; for, as is known, every organ in the body is supplied with nerves which, when overactive, produce effects deviating from normal. Suppose instead we now accompany John Doe, who is habitually very tense, in a typical attempt to find a better adjustment to life.

Perhaps Mr. Doe is one of the many harassed victims of tension today who seek a quick cure. He reads in newspapers, magazines and circulars how he can get well fast in two treatments. He pays his money and takes his choice! After taking the quick cure, he may be impressed if he feels better even for a few days or weeks. If not, come to think of it, he has watched yoga exercises on television, and he decides to give them a try! Like any other gymnastics, this kind may help his circulation a lot and perhaps lead him to believe that at last he has found it! He is no scholar of religions and does not know three things: first, that yoga has never been thought of as favoring muscular relaxation in the Far East, where it was originated and has been practiced by religious devotees for centuries past; second, that yoga favors relaxation has been sold to credulous Americans only since progressive relaxation has become known in America; third, that what yoga really stands for is to unite and yoke your soul to the world soul. Its aim is religious salvation through physical exercises.

Needless to say, salesmen of quick cures and of yoga exercises in America will not test their clients with our integrating neurovoltmeter to find out whether the improvement is real or just imagined. But any satisfied customers may not wish to be tested medically. "Where ignorance is bliss, 'tis folly to be wise!"

Perhaps Mr. Doe visits a very good doctor, who is accustomed to look chiefly for clear-cut pictures of pathological changes in tissues. The doctor concludes that there is nothing seriously wrong and refers the matter to a neurologist. This specialist makes another examination and, as before, finds "no pathology". The nerves are all structurally intact. He tells Mr. Doe, "There is nothing the matter with you. Go home and forget it!"

Mr. Doe tries to follow the advice. He feels relieved because both doctors have said that there is nothing seriously the matter. But the symptoms continue, or soon return, interfering with his work and happiness, and he begins to wonder what to do next.

Accordingly, Mr. Doe tends to go from physician to physician, feeling that he has not been understood. If told that his suffering is only imaginary, he becomes greatly puzzled, because to him it seems very real. Perhaps he comes upon a physician who maintains that nervousness always is caused by some organic disease and who discovers something that has previously been overlooked—for example, infected tonsils. Thereupon the tonsils are removed, and the patient awaits the clearing up of the many symptoms he has long endured. But this hope also may eventually be followed by disappointment. For it has never been proved that nervous irritability and excitement can result from infections in the absence of fever and distress.

To be sure, if John Doe has become thoroughly imbued with the *belief* that the various measures, whatever they are, have removed the cause of his long sufferings, his feelings may be so greatly affected as to result in some improvement in his general symptoms. But the same sort of relief is likely to follow if the doctor prescribes a sedative drug or sugar pills, telling the patient that he will get well. The effects of such suggestions as a rule prove transitory; and even when the patient asserts that he has recovered, you probably can with care observe signs of nervous irritability. Probably you soon find Mr. Doe again going from doctor's office to doctor's office. Removal of his appendix and gall bladder likewise fails to effect lasting improvement, although for a time he feels somewhat better, following a long rest at the hospital.

Patients of this type are such frequent visitors at medical offices and hospitals that in extreme cases their incessant complaints finally tend to bore their doctors. Lack of interest on the part of the doctor in the nervous complaints of the average patient, when no serious pathology has been found, is likely to send that person toward pseudoreligious cults and charlatanism. Patience is a virtue which the tense, overeager individual does not possess. In the market he tries to get rich quickly. Notwithstanding repeated losses he goes in again and again, always trying to hit the jackpot. Likewise if he has nervous symptoms, he tries to get well quickly, not alone going from doctor to doctor but also confidently engaging in publicized methods for quick improvement. Imported methods tend to attract a large following, even if temporarily. Acupuncture was widely publicized, but appears to be on the wane. Buddhistic imports, called "transcendental" or by any other name, prove attractive to many seeking a quick cure. Appealing to the impatient section of our populace, quick ways to become relaxed are enthusiastically presented in magazine articles and books by would-be authorities.

We can reasonably expect that various types of quick cures of tension disorders will follow one another to eventual oblivion. Like lotteries, they will continue to prove attractive to some. Nevertheless, the more prudent will recall that a college education cannot be gained in a day or even a month. In the long run the reality will dawn that thorough treatment of tension disorders likewise requires time for lasting results.

Many tense patients complain of symptoms which do not appear to them to have anything to do with the nervous system. Often the trouble seems to lie in some particular organ. One person has noted, for instance, frequent bowel movements with abdominal pain and perhaps with mucus in the stools for months or years. Another becomes constipated whenever he passes through trying situations. A third experiences a choking feeling in his throat, which interferes with his daily comfort and with his work and which is slightly relieved when he belches after taking soda. A fourth believes that he has heart disease since his heart sometimes beats very fast and hard and may even skip beats. Occasionally the complaint is frequent urination. Poor vision, in spite of a satisfactory report from the oculist, is often mentioned.

If Mr. Doe's symptoms continue, as seems likely, possibly he will find a doctor familiar with tension disorders. The story of an examination may run somewhat as follows: The doctor looks at Mr. Doe's scalp and hair and finds them practically normal. He shines a bright light on the pupils while Mr. Doe looks at a corner of the room, and they become small, as they do also when Mr. Doe looks at a pencil near by, which means that this test for syphilis of the nervous system is negative. The doctor looks into the nose and probably finds changes not considered important in the present connection. If infections appear in the teeth, Mr. Doe is referred to his dentist. The tongue may show a slightly grayish or yellowish coating. In excitable persons, examination of the tonsils and throat sometimes produces gagging. But touching the wall of the throat generally does not arouse any reaction in the condition technically known as "hysteria". While the patient swallows, the doctor's fingers glide over the neck; he finds that the thyroid gland is soft and of no unusual size and that there are no enlarged lymph glands. When Mr. Doe breathes deeply, his chest, let us assume, is seen to move freely in all its parts and maintains normal contour. The doctor now feels and taps the chest, outlining the heart and lungs. As he applies the stethoscope, he hears normal breath and heart sounds, aside from a quickened beat and perhaps a murmur, which he knows is not important.

After his patient lies down, his hand finds the liver and the spleen in proper position. If excited or fearful, the patient may be holding the abdominal muscles tense, interfering with the examiner's efforts to feel the contents of that region. In highly nervous persons, portions of the large intestine frequently are tender upon pressure and sometimes may be felt as a somewhat firm mass or a number of masses. Perhaps Mr. Doe has previously experienced a tenderness in the right lower portion of the abdomen, leading him to believe that he has chronic appendicitis. On this point the careful physician will not make a diagnosis until he has ascertained all the facts. Even if the appendix has been removed in recent years, there may be tenderness in the region mentioned. The doctor looks over the skin of the entire body and probably finds nothing of note, except perhaps flushing.

Using a rubber-tipped hammer, he lightly strikes certain tendons, including one below the knee, inducing a marked kick. These tests disclose whether the muscle involved and the nerves leading to the muscle are structurally intact. In many but not all nervous persons the kick is relatively violent, showing that the local nerve and muscle tissues are tense. If Mr. Doe is nervously excited during the examination, this may cause a little fever, as indicated by the thermometer. And if he is considerably worried about his blood pressure, the doctor may find it increased. I have seen a rise of sixty points in systolic pressure during such worry and a fall to normal within half an hour as the patient became relaxed. Accordingly, the diagnostician makes repeated readings in order to ascertain whether the pressure is characteristically high. In chronically fatigued persons it often is somewhat low.

Mr. Doe is again sent to the laboratory. Specimens are taken of his urine and blood. Perhaps he learns that they prove negative, or possibly that the number of white blood cells is above normal. This may indicate that he has an area of inflammation somewhere, but in some instances it means only that he was highly emotional at the time the specimen was taken. A series of chemical tests include blood cholesterol, calcium, urea, but also concern venereal disease. Routine X-rays are taken of his sinuses, teeth, heart and lungs. Let us assume that they prove negative. After he has swallowed a glassful of buttermilk containing barium, the doctor looks at the digestive organs. Wherever the barium appears, the X-rays cannot pass through, and so organs containing barium become clearly outlined. The X-rays are likely to disclose that the muscle walls of his digestive tract are contracted irregularly in various places, a condition commonly called "spastic".

Concerning the results of the examination, the doctor reports, "I agree with the physicians who have previously told you that there is no serious impairment in the structure of your nervous system or in other organs. But I cannot agree that there is nothing wrong with you and that your sufferings and inefficiency are imaginary. My observations disclose that as a rule too many of your muscles are contracting, not alone when you are busy but even also when you try to rest. This means that your nerves are overactive. You evidently are wasting energies in various directions with no good effect, and to this I would attribute the fatigue you complain of as well as your failure to secure sufficiently restful sleep. Furthermore, the X-ray examination definitely discloses that your digestive organs are overtense. My advice is that *you must learn to relax*!"

13

OVERACTIVE NERVES AND MUSCLES

"Tension disorder" is the diagnosis following the doctor's examination of John Doe, and "tension disorder" is the diagnosis on tens of millions of other persons trying to adjust to the complexities and rush of modern life. Perhaps Mr. Doe is greatly interested and sees a light ahead; but he does not fully comprehend what is meant by the diagnosis or why the doctor believes that he must learn to relax. Consideration of his case leads to various interesting questions: What is happening in the nerves of persons leading excessively wearing lives or suffering from painful or distressing diseases? Is there anything which the research laboratory can offer to the doctor to give him a picture of what is going on? If so, the opportunity arises to substitute something definite for the guesswork and speculation that has been rife for decades in the field of "functional" and psychiatric disorders.

What is meant by "excessive tension"? Before answering this, we recall that whenever you do anything, you contract muscles somewhere in your body. This applies equally to activities like breathing, which are essential to life, and to others, like talking, which often are better omitted. Every movement, then, depends for its occurrence upon the shortening of muscle fibers somewhere. Muscles compose about half of the weight of the entire body. Every muscle is supplied with a double set of nerves, one set bringing messages to the muscle, the other carrying messages from the muscle to the spinal cord and brain. Whenever the nerves coming to the muscle are active, the muscle they supply is active. This activity in nerve and muscle is chemical in nature. It proceeds along a nerve like a wave, at a rate of about forty to one hundred yards per second in man. The wave is also electrical in nature but, as just indicated, does not pass so rapidly as does electricity along wires, which moves as fast as light.

From what has been said, it will be evident that when a muscle contracts, electrical waves are present not only in the muscle but also in the nerves that lead to and from the muscle. We can often get a better idea of our organism by comparing it with a machine. When an automobile is in motion, its wheels turn according to its speed. At sixty miles per hour, they revolve about thirty times per second. Nerves discharge at rates per second, and so do muscles as shown when measuring instruments are applied. In muscles, as tension increases, the discharge varies from about one to 70 per second or more. Accordingly in persons who are spending too much energy, who think and behave tensely, we find many of their nerves and muscles are discharging more frequently than is best for health and accomplishment.

Nerve discharge into muscle, then, produces muscular contractions. This gives us a convenient way to describe overactive nerves or high nerve tension. It is the failure of the individual to be relaxed when and where he should be saving his energy.

An athlete running a race, a student writing an examination, a soldier at the front will naturally be in the state of high nerve tension. We should expect instruments attached to the muscles in action to record electrical discharges taking place at high frequency. But if the same individual lies down to rest and if no exciting conditions are present, we should not then anticipate that our instruments would record such discharges at high frequencies. Nevertheless, this is exactly what we frequently find in individuals who have been living overtense lives. Under conditions favorable to relaxation, recording devices show failure to relax. Nervous overactivity has become character-istic.

Can we be sure that persons who show nerv-ous overactivity have not some disease, discov-ered or hidden? Many patients (and some doctors) are inclined to assume that where there is abnor-mal "nervousness", there must also be some "physical" cause. Their reasoning is generally confused, since they commonly speak of nervous-ness as not being physical, whereas we have just seen that it has very definite physical characteris-tics. However, what they really mean is that to cause nervousness there must be somewhere a tumor or an inflamed tissue or a disordered glan-dular secretion. The evidence that nervous overac-tivity does not necessarily arise from pathological disease rests first on the common finding of care-ful diagnosticians that many persons are neurotic, although frequent examinations disclose no im-portant pathology; second, on the experience well known to all mankind that a succession of trying events or catastrophes obviously results in nerv-ous irritability and excitement; third, on the re-lief from nervous symptoms of persons in whom definite pathology exists but is not removed, when difficulties in their lives are cleared up by changed circumstances or when they have learned to relax.

On the other hand, without doubt, almost any severe disease tends to contribute to the develop-ment of nerve-muscle overactivity. Most commonly this occurs when there is marked or persistent distress or pain. Almost everyone has had the experience of becoming increasingly tense during protracted headache, toothache or colic. I have frequently tested this matter on normal subjects resting quietly upon a couch in the laboratory who previously have shown their ability to maintain relaxation. When a source of distress arose, such as headache or constriction due to a tight band used during an experiment, electrical currents were detected, indicating nerve-muscle overactivity.

Every physician has seen instances of nervousness arising from certain stimulating drugs or poisons taken by mouth. Such poisons also may be due to bacteria—for example, in certain stages of typhoid fever. Increased nervous activity is present during any condition of high fever and delirium; but it would be unwise to generalize from this that all bacterial infections, in all stages, are responsible for high nervous activity, because the matter has to be proved for each disease.

Owing to the distress and fear frequently associated with ailments requiring surgical treatment, patients often become increasingly nervous as the time for operation approaches. Following the operation, relief from the nervousness commonly occurs during a period of rest at the hospital. Both surgeon and patient should be cautious, however, in ascribing the nervous relief to the operation rather than to the enforced rest. In observing this caution, we do not minimize the importance of needed operations.

Occasionally patients relate that they have been nervous since an attack of food poisoning. They have vomited or had diarrhea. Unfortunately, we still lack tests for some types of food poisoning that probably exist. When a number of persons who have partaken of the same food fall sick at about the same time, the circumstantial evidence is clear. But when the patient suffers alone, has no fever and perhaps shows marked nervous symptoms in other respects, the symptoms may have been due to a nervous upset. In the absence of decisive evidence, no conclusion should be drawn.

Nervous overactivity is present in the disease involving the thyroid gland, called toxic goiter. In this condition there is no doubt that excessive or disordered secretion from this gland causes high nerve tension.

After an acute infection, such as influenza, there sometimes follows insomnia or nervous irritability. Whether this consequence is due to the action of bacteria or to the distress and fretting about symptoms and confinement may be impossible to say.

Defects or disabilities which tend to make it hard for an individual to get along in his environment contribute to the development of nerve tension. Examples include poor vision or hearing, stuttering or stammering, crippled limbs, deformities and mental subnormalities.

Evidently, then, sources of pain and distress may cause nervous overactivity. Stimulating drugs and bacteria producing fever may have the same effect. Inflamed and swollen tissues, stretching the ends of sensory nerves, undoubtedly create high nerve tension. However, where pathology exists, like a chronically abscessed tooth or tonsil or other organ, but with no distress or pain, we must not assume that here likewise is a cause of increased nerve tension. For many persons have such conditions without being excessively tense, and the removal of such diseased areas is not followed in them by any noteworthy change in their nervous reactions. When tales are told of remarkable recoveries from insanity or marked nervous disorder after pulling a tooth which had not been painful, we should be very skeptical.

Many children become nervous because parents are overattentive. They become stimulated like the actor in the play who knows that his every movement is being watched. Overstimulation in the evening hours after the father has come home is particularly obvious.

Enough has been said to give a general idea of some of the causes of nervous overactivity. Many patients relate that their nervous symptoms arose apparently because of worries. Frequently the concern is over one's own health or that of some loved one, but commonly it is over money matters. How general are such experiences is shown by the amount of attention given to this theme in novels. In Henry Handel Richardson's *Ultima Thule*, for example, the chief character, having lost his fortune and his friends and finally a child by death, undergoes an apparently increasing nervous overactivity and gives a lurid description of his sufferings: "To wake in the night, and to know that, on this side of your waking, lies no ray of light or hope . . . only darkness and fear. To wake in the night: be wide awake in an instant, with all your faculties on edge: to wake, and be under compulsion to set in, night for night, at the same point, knowing, from grim experience, that the demons awaiting you have each to be grappled with in turn, no single one of them left unthrown, before you can win through to the peace that is utter exhaustion. . . . The order in which his thoughts swept at him was always the same. The future . . . what of the future . . . ?"

Evidently the public is highly interested in the subjective phases of overactive nerves or high nerve tension and their causes. However, the chief purpose of the present volume is to disclose the objective phases and to discuss measures for their regulation or removal. We have concluded that nerves are overactive if they show evidence of electrical waves occurring at higher firing rates than they normally should. We note such evidence in anyone when his muscles are needlessly tense, whether during attempted rest or during activity. The causes of overactive nerves are various; but among these causes we particularly note the rush and complexities of modern living.

Listed above are some of the many varieties of hardship and disease commonly leading to overactive nerves. Whatever the cause, once a person has become too tense, his condition tends to be habitual. To break the habits, he will need to learn tension control.

14

TRANQUILIZERS AND SEDATIVES

Quieting of nerves is often attempted through the use of medications known as tranquilizers. Their manufacture has become big business. This shows how widespread is tension among our populace. Tranquilizers alone are being sold at the rate of one hundred and fifty million per year and the public demand appears to be growing.

With the demonstration that even vicious monkeys could be rendered calm and manageable for a time by the administration of forms of "snake-root", the use of tranquilizing drugs was dramatically introduced into the daily practice of medicine. Today the demand has become so great that (where laws permit) druggists commonly dispense them to customers without prescriptions. Sometimes they are known as "happy pills".

Without doubt, there are times and places where tranquilizing agents can prove of use to many psychiatrists. They are being employed to advantage in state hospitals, especially on patients who are irrational and out of contact with nurses and attendants. They have been publicized extensively and are easy to prescribe and easy to take. Thus they constitute a temptation to the busy doctor, especially if he has little time or has little interest in more thorough methods.

Objections to the use of tranquilizers when unwarranted and excessive are growing in frequency. They are being voiced by many doctors.

Dr. H. A. Dickel and Dr. H. H. Dixon have pointed to the danger to the physician which results from accumulating pressure on the medical profession from the people who produce and those who demand these drugs. They apparently have in mind that fears and anxieties play a necessary role in the constructive efforts of any society and therefore should not be completely silenced by stupefying drugs.

Medical journals issue warnings in their editorial columns against the abuse of tranquilizers. In a letter addressed to the president of the Foundation for Scientific Relaxation, the editor of a leading medical journal wrote, "I heartily approve of any efforts to combat the current wholesale drugging of the public, which many of us view with considerable apprehension".

It is known that many of these medications excite side reactions or complications which include jaundice, skin eruptions, asthmatic attacks, blood changes and toxic delirium.

This has led to a search for tranquilizers with the least side reaction. Several have been found which satisfy this demand, more or less. However, even to these, individuals differ, some observing ill-effects. It is claimed that the best of them do not make the patient soporific, but many users get drowsy nevertheless. When under the influence at their work, their powers are lessened. Drive is reduced to such an extent that they have been called "don't-give-a-darn" tablets. Upon discontinuing certain tranquilizing medication, Dr. F. Lemere found that some of his patients felt nervous and let down.

Physicians still frequently seek to quiet the nervous system not only by tranquilizers but also by sedatives. These include barbiturates, bromides and others. Both sedatives and tranquilizers commonly produce their effects by depressing nerve tissues. In using them, we should recognize that we are taking into our bodies substances which are toxic; in lay terms they act as very mild poison. By this action they temporarily depress and thus throw out of commission some portion of our effort-system.

Why should we thus depress ourselves when without resort to medicines we are capable of ceasing these same efforts? Surely a civilized people need not resort to "snake-root", barbiturates or other preparations to deaden efforts which result from their own initiative! A more direct and a healthier route lies open. Just as the shortest distance between two points is a straight line, so the shortest distance between making an effort and not doing so is direct scientific relaxation. Obviously this is an improvement on measures of self-depression by drugs.

Sedatives like bromides and barbiturates commonly produce a sort of dulling or deadening which more or less allays nervousness until another dose is needed. Long-continued use generally causes loss in effect, requiring increased dosage or change of medicines, and perhaps leads to dependence on the medicine. While sedatives doubtless are useful occasionally, particularly in certain acute conditions, many doctors, including the author, believe that they are now employed far too commonly.

Sedatives not only can prove habit-forming but often depressing to the spirits in their after-effects. I have often seen such results. The patient may be emotionally disturbed in consequence, and his judgment about the difficulties which he faces may be discolored and even pathological. For these reasons alone many doctors prefer to employ them sparingly or not at all.

Fortunately, there is more than one door open to the doctor who sets out earnestly to help the nervous, troubled, perhaps hypochondriac patient commonly seen in office practice. When he despairs of the pharmacological route, if he chooses, he can turn to physiological procedures which are direct and often no less effective. It has been shown that to calm the nervous, tense patient the doctor needs to understand the physiological measures which he employs no less than if he were employing medications. Thus he may be required to devote more time and study to the patient's needs than if he were merely to dash off a prescription. Reported results, however, suggest that often he may be well repaid for his efforts; and side reactions will not be encountered.

Physiological investigations make clear that tension states in man, including those which yield however partially to tranquilizing agents, always include temporary or lasting contraction in skeletal musculature. Furthermore, it has been learned that the skeletal muscular contraction reflects the purposes and efforts of the patient in meeting his problems and in trying to achieve success in what he is doing. If he takes time for it, including a detailed history of the patient's tribulations and aspirations, the doctor can learn much about these states of tension-efforts in his patient. His next step is to acquaint himself with the physiology of progressive relaxation methods and to apply them however meagerly to his patient. He will find that the patient himself is endowed with what my friend Oscar Mayer called a "built-in tranquilizer".

In considering the basic physiology, it is believed, he not alone comes to a better understanding of the tension-states which underlie his patient's symptoms; in addition, when he shows the patient that it is his own excessive efforts which are responsible for much stress and strain, he shows the way that leads directly toward relief. For we know that the tranquilizing drugs and indeed all sedatives produce their effect through toxic action on some portion of the brain-neuromuscular circuit, while physiological methods of progressive relaxation in no way disturb the circuit but leave it intact. Not alone directness of approach and freedom from side reactions would seem to favor the use of the physiological approach; but the evidence suggests that what the doctor teaches the patient as a way of living and of meeting his difficulties is likely to stay with him longer and produce more lasting effects than will any tranquilizer.

15

VACATIONS, RESTS, EXERCISES AND HOBBIES LEAVE YOU TENSE

Many persons claim that they "relax" by driving, gardening, collecting stamps, playing golf or by some other hobby. What they mean by "relax" apparently is vague in their minds; it certainly is not defined as in the present volume. They do not present evidence that they conserve their energies—namely, their adenosine triphosphate. Obviously, they do not even have knowledge of precise statements. They could not run a business, not even a small store, on such vague views, with no consideration of financial costs.

They do not know that their hobbies are

costly in energy. Sometimes the believers in hobbies and diversions include professors. One day the distinguished chairman of the department of athletics in a neighboring university visited my clinic, bringing me a complimentary copy of his book on kinesthesiology. As he spoke, he commented that his field was related to my own. I was pleased with his gift and thanked him accordingly.

His hobbies included golf. About one year later I read in the newspaper of his death from a heart attack which began on the golf course. Obviously, this professor might have done better than resorting to physical exercise if he wished to live successfully.

What I am saying is "Everything in its place!" Golf is for certain people but not including candidates for heart attacks. Personally, I have enjoyed playing tennis, however poorly. I believe that in my college days I strengthened my muscles by daily running a mile and a quarter and also by daily deep-breathing exercises (which, by the way, are quite out of place in learning to relax the respiratory muscles).

Clear thinking assigns proper places and objectives for different therapies of approach to different ailments. Collecting stamps, for instance, may be enjoyable to you but will not be the route to reducing your overweight. Physical exercises, including sports, are important for entertainment as well as for benefits of muscular development and of circulation. They belong in an organized lifetime, but they do not include each and every virtue. They cost energy, adenosine triphosphate; they do not save energy. Nevertheless, the cost may be well worth while, especially in a healthy person. However, an individual with coronary insufficiency, as in the case of the professor, should learn to save his heart through tension control rather than to expose himself to the energetics of golf.

For clarity, let me explain that I had the honor to be consulted about relaxed playing of golf many years ago by no less an authority than the distinguished sports writer, Grantland Rice. He called at my hotel in New York to quiz me on a game which I had never played. He continued his questioning for about ninety minutes. Indeed, as today the distinguished pitcher Mike Marshall exemplifies, tension-control instruction belongs in professional sports no less than it belongs in elementary-school education for all pupils.

Many of my patients, after becoming proficient in tension control for their various complaints of digestive, circulatory and other tension disorders, speak enthusiastically about their improved playing of golf, following their application of differential relaxation.

Indeed, one example deserves special mention. Toward the end of World War I, a patient from the United States Army described how his parachute had failed to open when he pulled the cord. He fell to earth and the parachute fell upon him and broke his back. Army surgeons saved his life, but severe chronic pain persisted, bringing him to our Chicago clinic. Following months of habitual progressive relaxation, he became largely free from chronic pain and, thus restored, chanced to visit a golf course for the first time in his life. There, while professionals watched, he played his first game. They were so impressed as to urge him to learn to play, which he did and became one of the outstanding golf professionals of the country.

Coming back to hobbies, then, clear thinking will assign them as well as physical exercises and sports to proper niches in life without employing them (as do many untaught people) as panaceas.

In brief, hobbies, diversions and amusements may afford pleasure but will no more demonstrably reduce tension disorders listed in Chapter 1 than they will cure diphtheria, cancer or amoebic dysentery.

Similar considerations apply to vacations which many people falsely assume are panaceas for all maladies, including their complaints in the field of tension disorder. Vacations provide a pleasing change of scene and occupation. Where they commonly fail is to effect even a temporary, much less a lasting, habitual saving of personal energy. As is well known, many people on vacations plunge into gaieties, into gambling and/or physical exercises, spending their energies in unaccustomed activities pleasurably but profligately.

Patients learning tension control should be

urged to continue their one hour of daily practice even during vacations. Otherwise, upon their return, they are likely to be found more tense than when they left their daily affairs.

The reason why hobbies, vacations, amusements and diversions fail to prevent tension disorders is because they consist of lavish energy expenditures. They do not save adenosine triphosphate as does professional tension control.

It is reasonable to ask an additional question: Why should a tense person need to learn progressive relaxation? Why not ordinary lying at rest for an hour or so daily and rely on the consequences?

The answer follows from a published study on patients not trained to relax but who had rested daily lying for an hour or more over periods of at least four to nine months. Measurements were made of muscle tension in the right biceps region in seven such patients before training to relax. Two were physicians, one a physician's wife. Notwithstanding their daily habits of rest, all of them reported that they were characteristically restless when lying down as well as when engaged in daily activities, and all of them agreed that they habitually failed to relax and did not know how to relax. The impression gained from their medical histories, their symptoms and their behavior harmonized with their reports that they failed to relax.

One example can illustrate the kind of findings in all. The patient was a surgeon first seen at the age of sixty-one. At the age of fifty-three his pressure had been 175 systolic over 113, diastolic, and the insurance company refused him life insurance. At the age of sixty-one, following his return to his Chicago practice, he had rested lying down daily at noon for one hour for eighteen months. These daily rests did not reduce his high blood pressure and constipation.

Before training to relax, measurements were made on his right biceps-brachial muscles while he lay on his back at rest. They showed tension—failure to relax. Following tension control training, similar measurements indicated improvement. The muscles were more relaxed.

This surgeon cooperated. Upon learning to relax, his blood pressure began to fall.

On April 27, 1940, before an hour of treatment his blood pressure was 160 systolic and 116 diastolic. He received instruction to relax an hour per day twice weekly and practiced as per instructions one hour daily.

Gradually his pressure values fell although he continued his strenuous surgical career. By July 1942 his pressure values had become characteristically lowered. For example, before treatment, on the twenty-eighth it was 135, systolic over 90, diastolic.

Like true love, the course of blood pressure improvement does not run smoothly. There were relapses, including when his wife died of carcinoma. He retired at eighty-eight.

When he was ninety-two-years old I visited him at his apartment in Chicago, where he lived with his charming second wife, and again a year later, when in the sitting posture I found his pressure to be 128, systolic, over 80, diastolic. When I asked whether he continued at tension control, he replied, "Relaxation practice has become a part of me." His mind was clear, he was free from nervousness and he lived happily notwithstanding a mild condition attributed to Parkinson's disease.

THE NEW CULTURE FOR THE TROUBLED WORLD

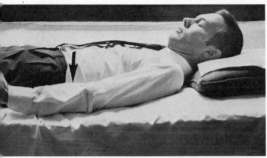

1.
While you bend your hand backward, you observe *tenseness* in the back part of the forearm.

2.
While you bend your hand forward, you observe *tenseness* in the front part of the forearm.

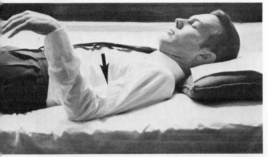

3.
Closing your eyes, bend your left arm steadily. You are to notice the sensation in the flexor muscles where the arrow points, which is called *tenseness*.

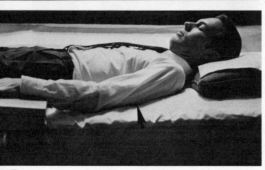

4.
As you extend your arm, pressing your wrist down against the stack of books (while your hand remains limp), you become familiar with *tenseness* in the extensor muscles, where the arrow points.

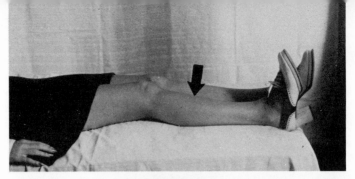

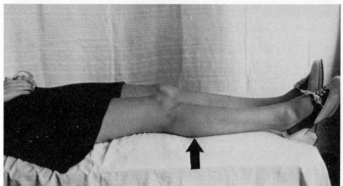

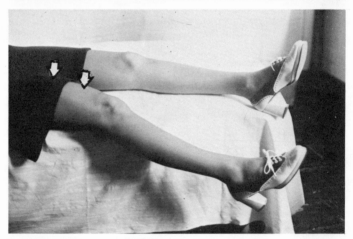

5. Bending your foot up, you observe *tenseness* in the muscles below the kneecap.

6. Bending your foot down, you observe *tenseness* in the muscles of the calf.

7. Extending your leg, you observe *tenseness* in the front part of the thigh. (Previously, while relaxing, with your leg over the edge of the couch, your shoe was nearer the floor.)

8.
Bending your leg (raising your foot backward), you observe *tenseness* in the back part of the thigh.

9.
Bending at the hip, with your left leg hanging limply over the edge of the couch, you should localize *tenseness* in the flexor (psoas) muscles, which are located deep in your abdomen toward your back.

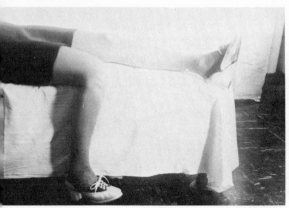

10.
Pressing down your heel against the floor, you observe *tenseness* in the buttock muscles.

14. Bending your head to the left, you observe *tenseness* in the muscles on the left side of the neck.

11. Drawing in the abdominal muscles, you observe faint *tenseness* all over the abdomen.

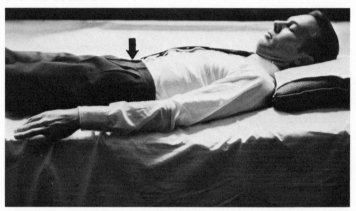

12. Arching the back, you should observe marked *tenseness* along both sides of the spine.

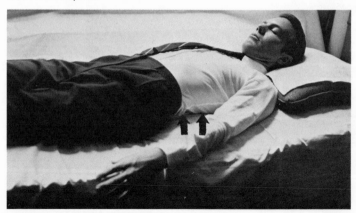

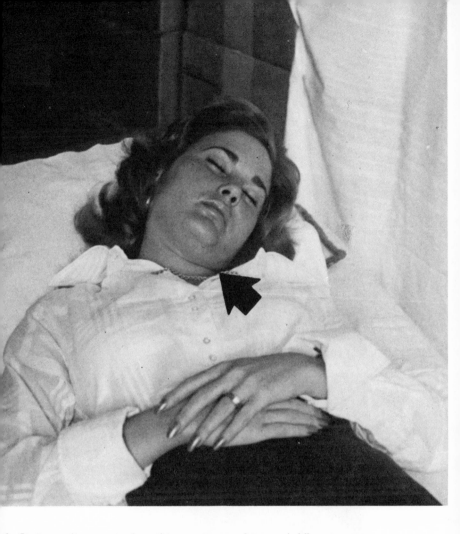

3. During ordinary quiet breathing, note very faint and diffuse *tenseness* all over the chest upon inhalation only; absent during exhalation and the pause which follows exhalation.

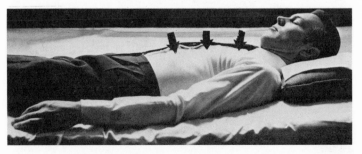

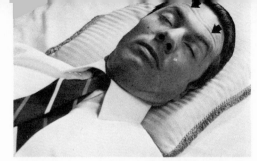

15.
Wrinkling your forehead is the occasion of *tenseness* diffusely over your entire forehead.

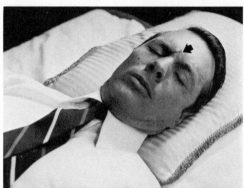

16.
Frowning can be felt distinctly in the region between the eyes.

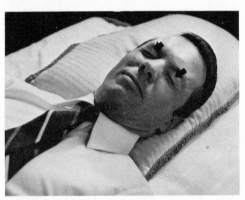

17.
Tenseness all over the eyelids can be observed upon closing them tightly.

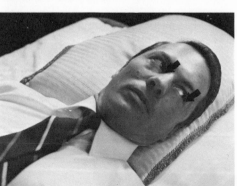

18.
Looking to one side, you should observe a sensation of *tenseness* in the eyeball muscles. Practice this with eyes closed until you get it distinctly.

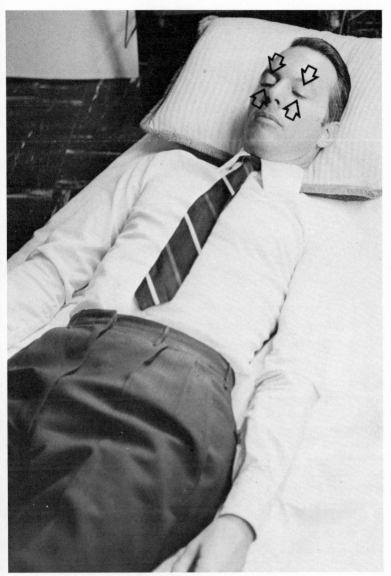

19. Looking from ceiling to floor, you should report that you see the ceiling and then the floor, and that you observe *tension* in the eyeballs in doing so. This *tension* changes rapidly as the eye moves, and for brevity is called a *moving tension* to contrast it with the fairly *steady tension* you experience when a muscle is held rigid as in Fig. 1.

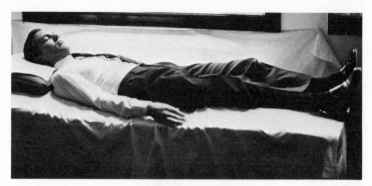

20. This illustrates complete *general relaxation*.

21.
In the sitting posture, you are to review all the *tensions* previously performed lying down. Bending the arm, you should be able to feel the *tenseness* very clearly.

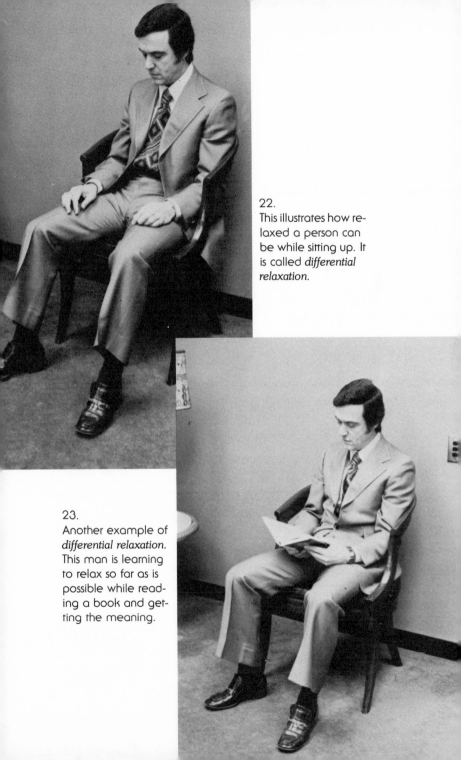

22.
This illustrates how re-
laxed a person can
be while sitting up. It
is called *differential
relaxation.*

23.
Another example of
differential relaxation.
This man is learning
to relax so far as is
possible while read-
ing a book and get-
ting the meaning.

24. At work, but *differentially relaxed*. He is saving his energy and is more efficient.

25. In the present studies, tension has become a measurable reality (replacing the vague use of this term commonly employed). Here is a young doctor learning to be relaxed as he sits at a desk. He is helped when he can see on the visioscreen just how tense he is at any moment in his forearm muscles. Platinum-iridium electrodes lie on his skin above these muscles. From these electrodes, wires pass to recording instruments developed in our laboratory.

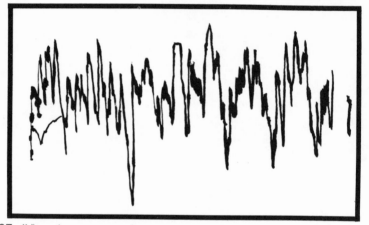

1 μv.

0.1 sec.

26. When a muscle region is relaxed or almost so, as measured with the integrating neurovoltmeter, this can be made visible with an oscilloscope (an instrument familiar in most electronic laboratories). The moving beam of light then traces an almost straight line, as shown in Fig. 26. The unit of measurement is indicated below the tracing, namely one millionth of one volt, measurable down to a tenth of even this minute voltage. The unit of time, as also shown, is one tenth of one second.

27. When the same muscle region of the same individual is tense, the moving beam of light oscillates up and down, as traced in Fig. 27. Units of microvoltage and of time are the same as shown for Fig. 26. These two photographs were made when surface electrodes were in place on the skin over the muscle site. (The degree of tension can be measured in millionths of a volt per one tenth of a second or other unit of time).

Wires connected these electrodes with the input of our integrating neurovoltmeter, the only present-day instrument capable of measuring the minute tension states of mental activities. To determine how tense a person is in any muscle region, the integrating neurovoltmeter also provides means of averaging the voltage per minute or other unit of time. These averages are recorded over half-hour periods with a digital computer run by Richard E. Lange. The tension is averaged and recorded from five or more regions simultaneously.

16

SCIENTIFIC RELAXATION

By relaxation in any muscle we mean the complete absence of all contractions. Limp and motionless, the muscle offers no resistance to stretching. For example, if your arm is completely relaxed, it can be bent or extended at the elbow by another person with scarcely more effort than is required to overcome the weight of your forearm; as if you were a rag doll, he encounters neither resistance nor aid when he moves your hand. In an individual lying completely relaxed, in the present sense, all the muscles attached to the bones are limp. These are called the "skeletal muscles". Whenever you make a voluntary movement you do so by contracting some skeletal muscle or some group of skeletal muscles. General relaxation means the complete absence of all such movement. It means also the complete absence of holding any part of your body rigid.

When muscles are completely relaxed, the nerves to and from these muscles carry no messages; the nerves are completely inactive. From electrical tests later to be described, it is certain that complete relaxation in any set of nerves means simply zero activity in those nerves.

Most physicians and laymen as well as some scientific workers commonly use the word "nervousness". It seems safe to say that although the term is often used vaguely, it always means that nerves in some part or parts are active. Employing this usage, we can restate what was said above. *It is physically impossible to be nervous in any part of your body if in that part you are completely relaxed.* The reader is urged to examine carefully the evidence and reasons for this statement as presented herein and if possible also in the more technical volume, *Progressive Relaxation.* He is requested to consider whether this statement, if true, implies that in complete relaxation we have, to a certain extent, a direct and specific treatment for what is frequently called "nervousness".

During general relaxation, even certain involuntary movements are absent; for instance, if a sudden noise occurs, the relaxed person shows no start. But we are anticipating; let us, instead, return to our story.

Since physicians have found rest useful, it seemed important to seek by scientific means the most effective form of rest. This brought to attention the fact that the patient advised to remain in bed often fails to get the desired restful effects. He may not know how to relax, and his restlessness may be increased by distress of one kind or another; therefore he may shift and fidget in bed, lie stiffly or uncomfortably, owing to tense muscles, and may be worried, impatient or otherwise overactive in mind. In effect, the physician's purpose in prescribing rest in bed may be nullified.

Strange to tell, what occurs during rest has generally been so little studied that even in well-known treatises on nervous disorders the word "relaxation" seldom appeared until recent years. It has been less neglected by followers of certain cults. Annie Payson Call, a follower of Swedenborg, helped persons (1902) to cultivate poise and to use "relaxing exercises". Her work seems in certain practical respects highly commendable. But her interests were not scientific and when she stated that an individual may remain nervous while relaxed by her measures, it is evident that she failed to study the extreme or finely drawn-out relaxation which is the essential aim of the present method.

In the course of laboratory studies presently to be described, a method to produce an extreme degree of nerve-muscle relaxation was gradually developed. What is customarily called "relaxation" was found in many instances to be inadequate and undependable for our purposes, both investigative and clinical. I found, as others had found previously, that an individual might lie on a couch apparently quiet for hours, yet remain sleepless and nervously restless. Even as he lay there, he might continue to betray signs of mental activity, organic excitement, anxiety or other emotional disturbance. He might breathe irregularly, fidget and start; might move his eyes, fingers or other parts of his body from time to time; or perhaps he might speak unnecessarily. These signs might occur occasionally or frequently and might either be quite obvious to the observer or require close inspection. When attention is once called to the matter, it is evident that such rest at best is not complete. Following it, the patient often fails to seem refreshed, retaining his symptoms and complaints of nervousness, fatigue or other ills. Accordingly, I was led to inquire whether the foregoing phenomena would not diminish or disappear if relaxation were cultivated to a greater degree and bodily extent.

It was evident that an extreme degree of relaxation was required, and for convenience I coined the term "progressive relaxation". The plan was to test whether excitement which has stubbornly persisted will tend under conditions favorable to progressive relaxation to give way to sleep and whether spells of worry or rage or other emotional disturbance will tend to pass off. A further development aimed to produce a certain measure of these quieting effects even while the individual continued at work or other activity. In substance, the hypothesis was that a method could be evolved to quiet the nerve-muscle system, including what is commonly called the "mind".

When the unpracticed person lies on a couch, as quietly as he can, both external signs and tests generally reveal that the relaxation is not perfect. There remains what I shall call *residual tension*. This may also be inwardly observed through the muscle-sense. Years of observation on myself suggested, in 1910, that insomnia is always accompanied by a sense of residual tension and can always be overcome when one successfully ceases to contract the muscles even in this slight measure. Residual tension, accordingly, appears to be a fine, continued contraction of muscle along with slight movements or reflexes. Often it is reflexly excited, as by distress or pain; yet even under these conditions relaxation is to be sought.

Doing away with residual tension is, then, the essential feature of the present method. This does not generally happen in a moment, except with certain well-trained subjects who are in practice. Frequently the tension only gradually disappears; it may take many minutes progressively to relax a single part of the body, such as the right arm. The desired relaxation may begin only when the individual might appear to an inexperienced observer to be very well relaxed.

Fatigued or nervous persons often fail to relax away residual tension. It is amazing how quietly such a one may appear to lie, while his arm or other part nevertheless reveals high nerve tension to the instrument used for recording this condition. Similarly, many persons who would not ordinarily be considered nervous or tense fail to relax completely.

When a person lies relaxed in the ordinary sense, but not completely relaxed in the physiological sense, the following signs reveal the presence of residual tension: his breathing is slightly irregular in time or force and perhaps he sighs occasionally; his pulse rate may be normal but is likely to be somewhat higher than that shown in later tests; the same is true of his temperature and blood pressure. If you watch him closely, you will see that he is not perfectly quiet, for he makes slight movements at times, wrinkles his forehead slightly, frowns, winks rapidly, contracts muscles about the eyes or moves the eyeballs under the closed lids, shifts his head, a limb or even a finger. The knee-jerk and other deep reflexes can be elicited (if there is no local nerve injury); he starts upon any sudden unexpected noise; in the studies undertaken up to date, if the esophagus or colon is spastic, it continues in this excited state. Finally, his mind continues to be active, and once started, worry or oppressive emotion will persist.

It is amazing what a faint degree of tension can be responsible for all this. The additional relaxation necessary to overcome residual tension can be slight. Yet this slight advance is precisely what is needed. Perhaps this again explains why the present method was long overlooked. As the individual relaxes past the stage of residual tension, his breathing loses the slight irregularities, the pulse rate may decline to normal, the temperature and blood pressure fall, the knee-jerk diminishes or disappears along with the throat and bending reflexes and the nervous start, the esophagus (assuming that the three instances studied are characteristic) relaxes in all its parts, and mental and emotional activity dwindle or disappear for brief periods. He then lies quietly with flaccid limbs and no trace of stiffness anywhere visible and with no reflex swallowing, while for the first time his eyelids become quite motionless and attain a peculiar toneless appearance. Tremor, if previously present, is diminished or absent, and slight shifts of the trunk or a limb or even a finger now cease to take place. Subjects independently agree in reporting that this resulting condition is pleasant and restful. If persistant, it becomes the most restful form of natural sleep. No university subject and no patient ever considered it a suggested or hypnoidal or trance state or anything but a perfectly natural condition. It is only the person who has merely read a description who might question this point.

High nerve tension, as shown in tenseness or exaggerated or excessive movements of the muscles which you move at will, presumably is subject to voluntary control. Every individual at least in some measure relaxes his muscles when he goes to rest. It would seem strange, therefore, if this natural function could not be specially cultivated to counteract an excess of activity and bring quiet to the nervous system. Such is the aim of the present method.

As may be readily noted, the overfatigued as well as the neurotic individual has partly lost the natural habit or ability to relax. Usually he does not know what muscles are tense, cannot judge accurately whether he is relaxed, does not clearly realize that he should relax and does not know how. These capacities must be cultivated or acquired anew. Accordingly, it is usually futile to tell the sufferer to relax or to have him take exercises to this end in gymnasiums. Following popular standards a patient may be apparently "relaxed" in bed for hours or days, yet be worried, fearful or otherwise excited. In this way at times the patient has been wrongly considered at rest, while voluntary or local reflex activities, as described above, have been overlooked. The detection of such signs is useful in diagnosis and in directing the patient or subject so as to bring about nervous and mental quiet.

According to my experience of 70 years in the clinic and in the laboratory, if the patient learns how to relax the voluntary system, there later tends to follow a similar quiescence of the internal organs, including the heart, blood vessels and colon. Emotions tend to subside as he relaxes. To be sure, there may be a vicious circle: visceral nervous overactivity seems to stir up the central nervous system, whereupon this system stirs up the visceral system still more. The one system must become quiet before the other system can become quiet. So in certain chronic cases, relaxation becomes a gradual process—a matter of habit formation that may require months. Various stimuli that occur during pain, inflammation or disordered glandular secretion, such as toxic goiter, may give rise to visceral muscle spasm and therefore hinder relaxation. Under these difficult conditions, it is traditional to assume—and patients often assert—that an individual "cannot" relax. Yet such inability would be difficult to prove. The presence of a reflex response to pain or other stimulus, as will later be shown, is not in itself proof that the reflex "could not" have been relaxed. This is precisely what needs to be investigated, for the patient's subjective views as well as the physician's *a priori* conceptions should not take the place of laboratory and clinical tests.

For clarity, it seems worthwhile to repeat what was said above, but in other words. Many persons ask, How is it possible to relax the stomach, the intestines, the heart or other internal organs? Can direct control be gained? The answer comes from experience in the clinical field as well as from laboratory tests, which indicate that *if you relax your skeletal muscles sufficiently (those over which you have control), the internal muscles tend to relax likewise.* You control the internal set to this extent, however indirectly, even without training. There is another way of looking at it. The person whose visceral muscles are overtense, as presented in certain states of nervous indigestion, spastic colon, palpitation and other common internal symptoms, shows clearly to any qualified observer that his external muscles also are overtense. Electrical measurements support this statement. If he relaxes the external muscles sufficiently—those under his control—the symptoms from the excessive internal muscular tension subside, while tests indicate that the internal muscles are no longer so spastic. This suggests clearly that excessive tension or spasticity in the visceral muscles depends more or less upon the presence of excessive tension in the skeletal muscles. If so, relaxation of skeletal muscles is effective in the treatment of certain internal disorders because it removes the cause, or an essential part of the cause.

After emphasizing the difference between "scientific" and "ordinary" relaxation, it is equally important to emphasize their fundamental identity. Under favorable conditions untrained individuals relax, as shown by recording instruments, although generally not so fully as after training. So-called phlegmatic individuals are particularly likely to succeed. It may be assumed, however, that whatever the natural propensities of an individual toward relaxation, there is always considerably more that he can be taught—just as anyone with a naturally good voice nevertheless improves greatly with proper training. In my experience persons who have not been trained to relax are less likely at times of emotional disturbance to resort to voluntary relaxation. They fail to apply the ability even if they have it; yet the process of relaxation, whether natural or cultivated, is essentially the same.

Experience has shown that for the convalescent who is not confined to bed there is no conflict in prescribing exercise to alternate with rest. The one prepares for the other, and the degree and extent of relaxation are likely to be increased after moderate exercise.

Before training any patient, the doctor will of course take a detailed history and follow this with thorough physical, laboratory and X-ray examinations leading to a correct diagnosis. He may find it necessary to employ surgery or drugs or hygienic measures in addition to progressive relaxation. Obviously it is important to remove, as far as possible, both physical and mental sources of difficulty and excitement. Since this ideal often cannot be realized, the method of relaxation will seek to reduce the nervous reaction even when the sources remain unavoidably active.

If the purpose in employing relaxation is investigation rather than practical results, other measures of treatment must be excluded as far as possible. However, even considering only the practical interests of the patient, it is best in many instances to exclude additional measures of therapy until the effects of relaxation have been thoroughly tested; for otherwise, if the condition should become improved, doubt would arise as to what agent was responsible for the result, and in consequence the wrong one might be selected for continued use.

For the same reasons it is frequently best to have the patient follow his usual routine in his work and social affairs, learning to relax in the very presence of his difficulties. If his program is made lighter while he is trained to be relaxed, and he eventually recovers, there will be no way to determine how much benefit should be attributed to the relaxation alone, and he may give relaxation too much credit or too little. In the latter event he will neglect to practice after he is once well and may suffer a relapse.

The importance of daily practice cannot be too much emphasized to anyone who seriously intends to cultivate habits of relaxation whether lying down or during normal activities. Obviously neglect of practice may mean the loss of much that has been gained up to that point.

When the relaxation is limited to a particular muscle group or to a part of the body, such as a limb, it will be called *local*; when it includes practically the entire body, lying down, it will be called *general*.

We call the relaxation "progressive" in three respects: (1) The subject relaxes a group, for instance the muscles that bend the right arm, further and further each minute. (2) He learns one after the other to relax the principal muscle groups of his body. With each new group he simultaneously relaxes such parts as have received practice previously. (3) As he practices from day to day, according to my experience, he progresses toward a habit of repose—tends toward a state in which quiet is automatically maintained. In contrast with this, experience indicates that the individual who indulges in unrestrained excitement renders himself susceptible to further increase of excitement.

Evidently an important thing to learn about yourself is how you spend your energies. Such spending occurs when you contract a muscle. But often you stiffen a muscle or move somewhat without being aware of it, and in some persons such "unconscious" expenditures of energy are found in clinical practice to be frequent or habitual. This suggests the need for an inventory. The ability to observe your tensions obviously should aid you in the attempt to diminish certain ones. No fear need arise that such observation will lead you to become morbidly aware of yourself; rather, in my experience, it leads quite in the opposite direction.

When we say that a person is "tense", we mean, in popular terms, that he is "high-strung". When we say that a muscle is "tense", we mean

that it is contracting—that is, its fibers are shortened. In addition, a third meaning of the term
"tense" is used in this volume. If you will go into
a quiet room, lie down and after a few minutes of
rest make some movement slowly and steadily,
you may, with practice, notice a sensation in the
muscle which contracts. This experience we agree
to call "tenseness". We agree also to call the same
experience wherever it appears in the body and
whatever its intensity by the same name. You are
not expected to be a physician or physiologist
when you learn to relax and therefore are not
expected to learn where your muscles are or what
they are doing. But it is necessary for you to learn
to recognize the sensation of tenseness. For this
enables you to know when and where you are
tense, in order that you may be able to correct the
condition if excessive.

As previously said, muscle tensions make up
much of the warp and woof of living. Walking,
talking, breathing and all of our activities involve
a series of complicated and finely shaded tensions
of various muscles. To do away with all such
tensions permanently would be to do away with
living. This is not our purpose, but at times we
need to control them, and relaxation is a form of
such control.

Learning to recognize and locate your sensations of tenseness is helpful, but is not invariably
needed, for relaxation often proceeds automatically without your bothering about it; and this is

always to be encouraged. If you watch your sensations and watch yourself relax continually or at a wrong moment, you will remain in a tense state. On the other hand, it is my common experience that some muscular regions frequently fail to relax completely until the subject learns to locate tenseness in them. A happy medium is reached when, with a minimum of attention, the disturbance is located and then relaxed. Moments of attention to muscles become increasingly unnecessary in the course of months as relaxation becomes habitual. This is like any other learning process, requiring less attention as time proceeds. After relaxation has been cultivated, it proceeds, at its best, automatically with little or no clearly conscious attention.

17

HOW TO RELAX
LYING DOWN

To learn to pass from the state of tension that usually characterizes modern living into one of marked relaxation within a few minutes or less; to repeat this again and again until relaxation becomes habitual—such, from the present standpoint, are the aims of tension control.

This is a course which many persons will take weeks or months, perhaps years, to complete. It is not reasonable to expect to alter habits with the speed of taking a pill or buying a theater ticket. But the matter is not so difficult as it sounds. In fact, it is not difficult at all; rather, it is the easiest of things to learn. To clarify this matter, stretch out your arm and lift a heavy weight with it. As your muscles contract, you find yourself exerting effort; you find that the lifting is difficult. But suppose that you do not bother to lift the weight, just letting your muscles relax. This is the negative of exertion, the negative of difficulty. Nothing could be easier. But many persons have acquired habits of exerting themselves in everything they do, so that they contract some muscle or other even in trying to relax. In this way they make difficult what is not naturally so. We call this the "effort error".

Serious ailments, as previously said, are best referred to the physician, who decides whether relaxation or other methods are most fitting. The physician experienced in methods of relaxation observes and treats the patient for periods of about an hour, repeating them as often as seems necessary. If the patient is greatly fatigued, sleepless or excited but has not been so for longer than a few days or weeks, he may learn enough from a few treatments to be able to return approximately to the same state he was in before the onset of the acute disorder. But if the malady has persisted for years, it is not reasonable to expect quick results; the method of relaxation is not magic; it does not, like hypnosis and suggestion, seek to accomplish its effects overnight. In chronic conditions, the physician sees the patient once a month or oftener, each time for about an hour, showing him how to recognize tensions and how to relax various parts of the body. After the patient has learned to be relaxed lying down, he is trained to relax while at work.

The patient practices by himself one or two

hours each day. Practice is indispensable, just as it is in learning to drive an automobile, to dance or to speak a language. With the aid of instruction, he achieves his own recovery. This is why the physician who uses the method of relaxation does not depend for therapeutic results upon inducing the patient to believe that he will get well. Indeed, even to accept a statement from the patient regarding his recovery would not be scientific; the only way to be really certain that recovery has set in is through objective observations, including laboratory tests. In other words, both physician and patient may entertain a reasonable skepticism without interfering with the method, provided that instructions to relax are carried out conscientiously.

The person who wishes to find out what he can do for himself should seek a fairly quiet room. In order to prevent intrusion by adults and children, it may be necessary to lock the door. Interruptions from the ringing of the doorbell or telephone or from other sources should be averted. For each period of practice, as a rule, about an hour of seclusion is best.

A comfortable couch or bed should be selected, sufficiently wide for the arms to lie on either side without touching the body. Generally a pillow is used to support the head. This is not necessary for persons who prefer to do without, provided that the head does not fall back, straining the ligaments of the neck and producing fatigue. To prevent this, at least a thin cushion is needed as a rule. In order to avert pain in rheumatic individuals, thin cushions may be used also under the knees or under the small of the back.

The best position for the average person until he has become expert is flat on his back—that is, he faces the ceiling. The reason for not lying on one side or with chest down is that generally such positions involve strain in some part of the body. Each arm in its entire length rests directly on the couch in such a way that the hand is at least several inches from the leg. Folding the hands is avoided since it gives rise to sensations of contact in the skin that are likely to prove slightly disturbing. For the same reason, the legs are not crossed. Accordingly, each portion of the body is supported practically directly by the couch.

While these preliminary instructions should be followed by the beginner, it is well to emphasize that relaxation can be achieved in any ordinary position. Persons who are learning to relax while lying on the back need not hesitate to go to sleep in any other position to which they are accustomed.

First Period

Under the conditions stated, lie quietly on your back for about three or four minutes with eyes gradually closing. Delay in closing the eyes permits a more gradual letdown. You should neither speak nor be spoken to. After this preliminary rest, bend your left hand back at the wrist. While so doing, do not raise the left forearm, including the left elbow, from the couch, where it should rest throughout the period. This is illustrated in Fig. 1. While this bending is maintained and your eyes remain closed, you should observe carefully a certain faint sensation in the upper portion of the left forearm. To give yourself time to become acquainted with this faint sensation, continue to bend back steadily for several minutes. This sensation is the signal mark of tension everywhere in the body. It deserves your interest, for it can prove of daily help to you. Vague as it is, you can learn to recognize and to distinguish it from other sensations. This will enable you to know at any moment when and where you are tense.

Do not confuse this vague sensation which marks tension or tenseness with that other sensation which is at the wrist. When the hand is bent at the wrist joint, vague sensations arise in this joint which we call "strain". Strain sensations are merely the passive results of your effort; they are more conspicuous as a rule than are sensations from muscle known as "tenseness" and often obscure these more important sensations.

Accordingly, the sensation experienced when a muscle contracts is to be called "tenseness". Note that this experience is dull or faint and is readily obscured. It differs in quality from the pain produced by pinching the muscle, from tickle, from touch produced by the application of cotton to the skin and from sensations of warmth or cold. If you scratch yourself with a pin or a pencil, you have an example of a sensation that is well outlined. But when a muscle is tense, the limits of the sensation are generally ill-defined, and the experience is diffuse. Tenseness, when moderate, is neither agreeable nor disagreeable but is particularly indistinct and characterless. To become familiar with the experience of tenseness so that it can be recognized wherever it occurs in any portion of the body is highly important in learning to relax.

During the first few periods we concern ourselves only with the left arm, neglecting tensions from other parts. In order for you to become familiar with the sensation of tenseness upon your bending your hand back, the action must be sustained. Be sure to bend steadily. Do not bend, then extend, then bend again irregularly. Such wavering motion or "seasawing" will fail to produce the steady sensation of tenseness which is desired in order to make you acquainted with the experience.

While observing the muscle-sense, you can observe better if you will keep your eyes closed. (People often close their eyes thus in order to note some delicate experience, such as a faint fragrance.) You will not need to learn where your muscles are located, nor should you feel them with your fingers when they tighten during contraction.

Some persons are slow in the cultivation of the muscle-sense. They generally are retarded in gaining the fine control of relaxation which comes to those who learn to recognize their muscle sensations. But even without this ability, a fair if not a complete measure of relaxation may be attained. It pays to be patient, to try again and again to recognize these sensations. For on the second or third day you may be able to note readily what seemed extremely vague and doubtful at first.

When you are satisfied that you clearly perceive the sensation of tenseness upon bending the hand back, you may realize, "This is you doing! What we wish is simply the reverse of this— namely, *not* doing!" Thereupon you are to discontinue bending the hand back, which should permit the hand to fall by its own weight. You can notice that the sensation called "tenseness" diminished or disappeared from the forearm region. It is agreed to call the disappearance or absence of this sensation "relaxation". We have defined the chief words, which we are to use, in terms of your experience.

As you relax the muscles that have bent your hand, you begin to learn clearly what it is *not to do*. You begin to realize that relaxation is not subjectively a positive something *but simply a negative.* After you have relaxed your arm for several minutes to illustrate this point, bend back the hand once more and then relax again. This time you are to observe that the relaxation involves no effort: you did not have to contract your arm or any other part in order to relax your forearm. These are important points to learn, for the untrained individual who fails to relax will contract various muscles in a vain effort to succeed. *Make certain that you do not pull your hand down to the couch with a jerk when you let go; also that you do not move it slightly after it has reached the couch in order to make it comfortable.* Such motions are often made by the beginner, who believes that he is relaxing; but they are unnecessary and definitely are contrary to methods of relaxation.

Bending your hand back again, you note that this is *effort*. But ceasing to bend your arm, relaxing it properly, involves no effort. It is important to realize that relaxation never is "hard" and cannot be; it is either done or not done, and that is all.

When these matters have been understood, bend back the hand again and let it go. Upon discontinuing this act completely, the hand should fall limply. *Do not actively move it back to its former position. Lowering the hand instead of letting it fall limply is a mistake made by many.*

As you will readily understand, *bending the arm is not a "relaxation exercise".* Bending at the wrist or any other act does not produce relaxation.

The acts illustrated in the figures are performed solely in order to create examples of what you are not to do when you relax. Contraction does not increase the relaxation present before the contraction. Physical exercise is the opposite of relaxation. It is doing something muscular, a positive act. Relaxation (going negative) is the reverse.

Following these preliminary attempts to recognize the sensation of tenseness, permit yourself about half an hour for continuous relaxation. *Do not continue to contract from time to time during the period*, or you will destroy the benefits from this relaxation. After contracting several times as directed, you are to devote the entire remainder of the hour to complete rest, avoiding any movement whatsoever, yet not "holding yourself still".

After you have recognized contraction in a muscle group, you can practice relaxing it completely. You are to learn to recognize contraction in the various parts of your body in a certain order. The large muscles are studied first, because the sensation therefrom is most conspicuous. As you relax a given part, you *simultaneously* relax all parts that have received practice previously.

Second Period

On the following day it is well to have a second period of self-instruction. As previously, your arms are to rest beside you, not in contact with your clothes. Begin by letting yourself become limp on the couch in order to prepare yourself to recognize faint muscular sensations, which otherwise might be obscured by other sensations. After about ten minutes of rest with eyelids open at first but closed later, bend your left hand back as you did the day before (Fig. 1), noting the sensation in the muscles in the upper portion of the left forearm. Then discontinue bending, letting the muscle rest completely for several minutes. Following this review of yesterday's practice, bend the left hand forward at the wrist as shown in Fig. 2. Continue to bend steadily while you try to locate the feeling of tenseness. It may elude you at first, but continue to try to observe it. *Do not seesaw, but maintain the tension steadily.* Eventually you should find it in the lower portion of the left forearm, as shown by the arrow in Fig. 2. But give yourself a chance to find it before you look for the location shown by the arrow.

Be sure to distinguish the sensation of tenseness thus recognized from the sensation of strain in the wrist.

Having observed the sensation during about one minute of steady bending, cease to bend. Go negative. This means what it says: do not make any effort to restore your hand to its former position. Such an effort would not be relaxing but would be tensing. *Every effort to relax is failure to relax.*

You are to bend your hand forward three

times (no more) during this hour of practice on the second day. The bending should be maintained without seesaw for about one minute for observation time. Between each act of bending, allow an interval of about three minutes during which you are to remain relaxed in the forearm.

After the third (final) bending, the forearm (and the remainder of you) is to remain relaxed for the remainder of the period. Accordingly you are to avoid bending again, letting your muscles relax as completely as you know how during the final half hour of the practice period.

Third Period

Instructions for the third period are most simple. Begin as previously, lying on your back with eyes open for several minutes; then let the eyes close gradually and do not reopen them, because no tension is to be performed. Your aim will be to maintain relaxation in the left arm—nothing more. This will require you to note the onset of tenseness, should this occur at any moment in the left upper arm. If it begins, you may be able to detect it, however slight and invisible, and to relax it, for it is *you* doing something. You are responsible for any shifting that arises, and, whatever your excuses, you are to avoid it. Simple as are the instructions, you will be entitled to a good mark if you carry them out successfully.

Fourth Period

In the fourth period, begin as you did on the previous occasions. After your eyelids have been closed for a brief interval, repeat the movements performed in the first and second periods. That is, bend the left hand back at the wrist for about one minute, observing carefully once more the sensation from tenseness in the upper portion of the left forearm, in contrast with the strain at the wrist and also the strain in the lower portion of the left forearm which you may now discern. Having done so, go negative. The hand should drop limply and relaxation should be maintained for several minutes. Thereafter bend the left hand forward at the wrist, observing as you do so the sensation from tenseness in the lower portion of the left forearm, in contrast with strain at the wrist and also the strain in the lower portion of the left forearm which now may have come above the horizon of your perception. Having observed thus, go negative for several minutes.

In following the directions given in this book, do not attempt to be precise in timing your acts of tensing or the periods of relaxation. When you are to bend back your hand for about one minute or are to relax thereafter for several minutes, do not perform by the clock or your wrist watch. It is better to estimate the time, for there is no need to be accurate in this.

Another precaution: Do not review more than three acts of tension in any hour of your practice. If you continue to tense one part after another (as many have done wrongly), you will fail to learn to relax because your hour will be devoted instead chiefly to physical exercises.

After the preliminary review, you are ready to begin your new task of the day. As shown in Fig. 3, bend your left arm at the elbow (to an angle of about thirty degrees), letting the hand drop limply at the wrist. In doing so, take care not to raise the left elbow from the couch. Remember to keep your eyelids closed during the entire hour of practice, except only during the beginning few minutes.

While bending the left arm at the elbow, look for the faint sensation of tenseness in the front part of the upper arm (where the biceps muscle is located).

If you are having difficulty in recognizing tenseness, the reason probably is that you are looking for too much. The sensation is delicate and you should adapt yourself to this fact. Do not look for a striking sensation, such as pain or even strain. If you wish, you may ask someone to hold back the forearm while you are bending at the elbow. This will intensify the sensation from the biceps region. But prepare yourself to discern sensations from muscular regions in the future without similar measures of reinforcement.

After discerning or failing to discern the sensation from tenseness during the act of bending for about two or three minutes, go negative. The forearm, including the hand, should fall limply as if this portion of you were a rag doll. Maintain the negativity for about three minutes. Then bend at the elbow once more for about one minute to allow for observation, after which go negative for several minutes. Thereafter bend at the elbow a third and final time for about one minute to allow for observation once more, after which go negative and remain so during the final half hour.

Fifth period

In the fifth period (on the fifth day), follow the procedure illustrated in Fig. 4. Your wrist is to rest on one or two books in thickness about four inches or a little more. The books may remain in place throughout the hour. You may omit the review of tensions observed in preceding periods.

In this period, begin as usual with eyes open but closing gradually. Once more, be sure to keep the eyes closed thereafter during the entire hour period. After the eyes have been closed for several minutes, press the wrist gently against the books while noting the sensation from tenseness now in the under surface (the back part) of the upper arm. Do not be confused by the strain in the forepart or in the elbow.

Following the order of procedure employed previously, observe the sensation from tenseness (for several minutes or less) three times in all. Go negative each time following the observation. Devote the last half of the period (like all other periods) solely to relaxing. This means that you are then to omit all movements whatsoever.

Sixth Period

Period six, like period three, is to be devoted from the very outset to relaxation alone, omitting all deliberate tensions.

Seventh Period

By the seventh period you may have become familiar with the sensations from the chief muscles of the left arm. Now is the time for you to experience that a part need not be moved in order to become progressively relaxed. While your arm continues in contact with the couch, stiffen the muscles so that the entire arm becomes rigid, but do not move it in any direction. Begin by making these muscles a little stiff and gradually increase more and more for about thirty seconds. After reaching a maximum do not contract quite so much as before, then a little less, still less, and so on and on, past the point where the arm seems perfectly relaxed, and even further. This is what is meant by "going in the negative direction". Here, then, is the type form of progressive relaxation for all muscular regions. Whenever in the early stages of practice you believe that you have completely relaxed some part of your body, you may safely assume that you are mistaken and that the part is at least slightly tense. Some degree of residual tension probably still remains, and your task is to do away with this entirely. Therefore, after you have ceased to hold your arm rigid until the point has been reached beyond which you seem unable to go, *whatever it is that you have been doing up to this point, continue that on and on.*

The warning is here repeated that one part of the above-mentioned illustration is not to be followed in the future. As a rule you should not stiffen the arm or engage in some other contraction before you relax but should begin to relax at whatever stage you find yourself. Graphic records have revealed that subjects sometimes fail to reach extreme relaxation because they contract at the moment they try to relax. If it is poor practice to contract every time before you relax, evidently steps should be taken toward preventing this from becoming a habit. Accordingly, not only are you to omit all tensions in practice periods number three and six, but similarly in periods number nine, twelve, fifteen and subsequent multiples of three.

Another warning of great importance is that you should not try to aid relaxation by repeating such sentences as "Now my arms are becoming numb!" or "My limbs are feeling heavy!" or "This is doing me good!" You are not to give yourself suggestions but are only to learn to relax just as you might learn to dance or swim.

If you have met with fair success in recognizing tensions, you may at the seventh period or somewhat later be made familiar with what I shall for brevity call *diminishing tensions.* You bend your arm, as shown in Fig. 3, noting the sensation of tenseness in the biceps. The bending is repeated halfway, then half of this and so on. A point is soon reached at which you are to bend it so slightly that an onlooker could scarcely note the movement. If you are still able to note the tension, you are to bend it again, but a little less, so that no movement would be outwardly discernible. Patients report (and electrical measurements confirm) that the experience of muscular contraction is again repeated but is considerably fainter than before. If you seem to confirm this finding, you are to bend again but still less than before. After several diminutions from this stage, the experience vanishes.

No one can learn to control his relaxation who does not know the difference between what we call "tenseness" and "strain". This test arises, for instance, when you bend your left hand backward in an attempt to locate the sensation called "tenseness". A common mistake is for you to point to the top of the wrist, where a tightness or pressure attracts attention, and to fail altogether to note the fainter sensation of tenseness which is in the upper portion of the forearm (see Fig. 1). If you make this mistake, you are requested to keep the left hand relaxed at the wrist while someone bends it back. You can then note the same tightness or pressure at the wrist as previously, when you were bending your hand backward. If observant, you will decide that these sensations at the wrist are by no means the same as the experience which it was agreed to call "tenseness". They are more definite in character than "tenseness", are more clearly outlined and, in general, feel different, just as warm differs in feeling from cold, tickle from touch, or pain from the other sensations mentioned. Accordingly, it is important to distinguish the sort of sensations noted at the wrist by another name, such as "strain". While your hand is bent backward without effort on your part, try to relax the strain at the wrist. You will fail, for the strain is not you *doing*, although it is often present and under favorable circumstances may disappear when you relax. If, while your hand continues to be bent backward by your assistant, you bend it backward still further by an additional effort of your own, "tenseness" now makes its appearance on the top of your forearm, whereupon the distinction should become apparent. When you relax your hand, the "tenseness" gives way to relaxation, but the strain at the wrist continues while your assistant bends back the hand.

In this manner you discover that sensations of tenseness are readily overlooked because of their relative faintness. These sensations are sometimes "unconscious" in the sense that they are commonly overlooked. Without doubt, in this sense, "unconscious" experiences can be relaxed away.

Another distinction to be learned is between experiences of *moving* and *steady* tensions—that is, changing muscular contractions versus rigid states. Flexion of the arm is an instance of a moving tension, while holding it rigid illustrates a steady tension.

Other muscle groups should receive practice in the preceding manner with variations according to your particular needs. Practice is devoted to the right arm in the same manner as described above for the left. After about twelve periods you may have completed both arms, but it would doubtless be better to spend about twenty or thirty periods up to this point. When you have learned to recognize tenseness in any muscle group—for instance, the biceps—it is well to permit a few days to elapse, during which your daily practice concerns only this muscle group, while from time to time as you go about your affairs you bend your arm for an instant, noting the sensation and localizing it. This will require very little loss of time from other matters, but you will have the benefit of many repetitions. As in seeing a particular face over and over again, you gradually become very familiar with the experience of tension in a particular region and can recognize even its faint forms with a minimum of effort and attention.

Relaxing the Legs

You are to learn to recognize tension in six muscle groups in each leg: Bending the foot or toes toward your face causes tenseness, not at the ankle or instep but in the front of the leg somewhat below the knee (Fig. 5). Bending the toes or foot down gives tenseness, not near the ankle but in the calf (Fig. 6). The experience of tension in the thigh can be brought out clearly if, during periods sixteen and seventeen, you lie in such a way that your left leg hangs limply over the side of the couch throughout the hour except when you perform the tensions. If the couch (or bed) is fairly high, your foot will not reach the floor. Extending (straightening the leg) should be performed as in Fig. 7, with the foot limp at the ankle joint. Your tendency will be to hold it rigid there. Maintain the posture shown in the figure until you clearly recognize the sensation of tenseness in the front part of the thigh. Bending the left leg as shown in Fig. 8 arouses the sensation in the rear part of the thigh. Bending the thigh upward arouses sensations deep in the abdomen in the hip region (Fig. 9). In order to bring out the experience the leg should be relaxed at the knee, so that the heel moves limply along the couch as the thigh bends.

Extending the thigh downward against a stack of books on the couch arouses sensations of tenseness as high up as the region of the buttock, where patients frequently overlook it (Fig. 10).

If at this or at any other stage aiming to relax seems difficult or "trying", you may be certain that this is because you are contracting somewhere. Probably you are making the "beginner's error"—that is, making an effort to relax. On the other hand, it is a sign of progress when you begin to enjoy giving yourself over to rest.

Subjects often report that complete relaxation is accompanied by no particular conscious feeling at all. Rather, they say, various sensations seem to fall away from a part as it becomes fully relaxed. One reports, "After a period of time I am no longer aware where my arms lie with regard to my body. The sense of location has lapsed."

On the other hand, if upon practice you feel "as if separated from your body" or have any strange sensations at all, pleasant or unpleasant, you are not relaxing as here taught. You had better stop altogether for the time being and begin again another day.

Relaxing the Trunk

We pass now to the trunk. You are to draw in the abdominal muscles, producing a diffuse experience of tenseness, readily noted over the entire front of the abdomen (Fig. 11). The same experience arises there if, after you have been reclining on your back, you bend up and forward. Bending backward (arching the back, Fig. 12) is accompanied by tenseness along the spine on either side. You should relax for a half hour before you try to localize tenseness in the muscles of breathing (Fig. 13). Then, during ordinary quiet breathing, note carefully a faint sensation all over the chest wall while you breathe in but not present while you breathe out. Patients sometimes wrongly state that they experience the tenseness in breathing solely under the chest bone and solely for the period when the breath is held. The way to relax your chest is precisely as you relax your arm— letting the breathing go by itself. "Controlled breathing" is not used as an aid to relaxation in the present method. Rather, the aim is to free the respiration from voluntary influence.

Various cults and various religious practices of the Orient, including yoga, make a feature of "breath control". The practices mentioned are mystical or religious rather than scientific and in my opinion are to be avoided by persons who consider their health first. In many instances they include hypnotic or hypnoidal states. However sincere the practitioner, a psychological understanding of what is performed is generally lacking. Suggestions and autosuggestions are given without clear realization of the fact. There can result injury to the personality, particularly the autonomous regulation of energies, to which this volume is dedicated.

Relaxing the Shoulders

After practicing relaxation of the breathing muscles, you come to the shoulders. In connection with each shoulder, recognizing tensions is of importance in three regions. Extending the arm forward and inward is accompanied by tenseness in the front part of the chest adjacent to the arm. Moving the shoulders backward and toward the spine is accompanied by tenseness between the shoulder blades. Shrugging the shoulders is accompanied by tenseness at the top of the shoulders and in the sides of the neck.

Relaxing the Neck

To become acquainted with tensions in the neck, you incline the head to the left (Fig. 14), to the right, forward and backward, noting tenseness respectively (chiefly) in the left side of the neck, in the right side, in the front and both sides and in the back of the neck. After each location has been recognized at the beginning of a period of practice, the remainder of the period is devoted to ceasing to make that contraction even in the slightest degree—"letting the head fall limply, like a rubber ball".

Relaxing the Eyes

The ability to relax the eyes, including the brow and lids, is a crucial test of skill. It is easy for most persons to distinguish tenseness in wrinkling the forehead (Fig. 15). The experience is located beneath the wrinkling skin. This region is then permitted to flatten out. Patients sometimes report that they can distinguish the sensations as they diminish for periods of many minutes. After frowning (Fig. 16), the brow likewise is gradually unfurrowed. You must take care that you do not wrinkle your forehead in trying to smooth your brow. If you make this mistake, you must try again, for you should learn that *it is not necessary to move in order to relax*. Next in order, the lids of the closed eyes are shut tightly, and tenseness is noted in the lids (Fig. 17). Gradually let the lids go, until winking of the closed lids has become infrequent or absent. At the next period look to the left with eyelids closed and note the tenseness in the eyeball region (Fig. 18). Observe again, looking to the right, later up and down. Look straight forward, noting the static tension in the eyeball region. Each movement or act is repeated until the experience is clearly discerned. Then let the eyes go completely, *just as you let the arm go*. You are not to try to look in any direction. If you fail to relax the eyeballs, stiffen your right arm and then gradually let your arm and eyes relax together. As a rule many repetitions are needed.

After a fair measure of success, open the eyes.

Observe what takes place in the region of your eyes as you look from ceiling toward the floor and back. You will experience a transient sensation of tenseness. Repeat several times so as to bring the experience to your attention vividly. You are using the eyes to look, and the sensation of tension can be a direct indication to you (if you learn to observe it) of the slight expenditures of energy involved.

There is more than one reason for your interest in this. In the past you have used your eyes with no awareness of how much at any time. If you would avoid overuse of the eyes, a first step is to become acquainted with means to recognize the muscular tension present whenever they are used, whether much or however slightly. In following the objectives and the directions of this book, you are seeking to save yourself from unnecessary use of your energies, in order to reserve those energies for things most worthwhile in life. In this objective, the eyes deserve special consideration, for they trigger the expenditure of energies over your entire body. This is because what you see (or imagine you see) determines largely what you do.

Try to become familiar, then, with the tension present in eye motion. Note also the *steady tension* present when you look at a fixed point in front of you perhaps five to ten feet away. Distinguish the sensation of tenseness from the sensations from burning and from strain. These sensations are more readily recognized, but they only result from activity; they are passive, like a broken arm. Tension is more important, for it is *you* doing.

Whenever you are in doubt what tension should mean to you, whether in the eyes or any other region, bend back your hand at the wrist. Thereupon notice once more the sensation in the upper section of the forearm which we know as tension. This will keep the experience fresh.

Relaxing Mental Activities

Many persons complain that "the mind keeps on working" after they lie down to relax, preventing sleep. Some even inquire in advance whether muscular relaxation will quiet the mind. The answer to these complaints or queries is for you to find from your own observations. Thus prejudice is avoided. *At no time should you make an effort to stop thinking or to "make your mind a blank". Throughout the course your sole purpose is to relax muscles progressively, letting other effects come as they may.*

For the following matters you will need a particularly quiet room, free from even such slight disturbances as the sounds of footsteps or of rustling papers. After about fifteen minutes of complete or almost complete relaxation of all the regions which have so far received practice, with eyelids closed, you are to imagine that you see the ceiling and then the floor of the room in which you are lying. If you succeed, you may note sensations of tenseness about the eyeballs like those which you experienced previously when with open eyes you looked from the ceiling to the floor. These sensations are sometimes readily recognized, but in many instances they are so slight that frequent repetition is required. After engaging in imagination as above indicated, you are to relax your eyes completely for five to fifteen minutes. Next you are to imagine seeing the wall on your left side and thereafter the wall on your right, making your observation. Practice imagining each wall successively until you become skilled in observing the tensions present when you imagine. Upon relaxing your eyes, visualization ceases.

At the next period of your practice you will again allow a preliminary interval for becoming relaxed. Thereafter you are to imagine a motorcar passing. If you are quick enough at observation, you will probably note a flashlike visual picture of a motorcar accompanied by a slight sensation of tenseness in the region of the eyeballs, as if the eyes are turning to follow the car. If you fail to make the observation, you should relax and repeat the experience. Some persons report that they lack clear visual images, noting the tenseness as if to follow the car but not seeing a car in imagination. If you have been successful, you are to imagine (with intervening periods for relaxation of the eyeballs) various other simple objects, moving or stationary, such as a train passing, a bird flying, a flower fluttering in the wind, a tall tree or tower, a ball rolling on the ground, a triangle, a square, a circle, a point, a blade of grass and a sailboat in the distance. As you gain skill in noting slight ocular tensions, you may assign yourself a more complex task, such as observing the experience when you recall the morning newspaper or when you perform a simple problem in arithmetic or when you think of some social or business matter. In each case, as a rule, following adequate training at observing, most persons report that their visual images are accompanied by sensations in the eye muscles as if from looking at the object imagined.

As far as possible you should not assume that this book is correct in stating that eye tensions accompany visual images but should test this matter for yourself. In medical practice, the physician does not even hint to the patient that he is to look for tensions during visual imagination—for leading questions are omitted where it is desired to conduct an investigation scientifically. Even if the desire is only for therapeutic results, it is better to have the patient rely on his own observations.

The instruction which you are to follow is to "cease to move the eyes in any direction or to look forward, yet not to hold them still: you are to relax the eyes in the same manner as you relax the biceps".

Upon relaxing your eyeballs completely,

avoiding such slight tensions as take place even during imagination, you will doubtless find that the mind ceases to be active. This, then, is a desired form of mental control.

We now pass on to other muscular regions, recalling again that one such region is enough for practice at any particular hour period. If you are unsuccessful at observing tenseness in any region, it is best to relax as completely as possible for a few minutes before repeating the experience.

Relaxing the Speech Muscles

Upon closing your jaws tightly, you should note tenseness extending from the angle of the jaws up to the temples. Opening the jaws produces tenseness which you may locate approximately in front of the ears but deep within the tissues. You are to show your teeth, noting tenseness in the cheeks (not in the lips, where there is a different sensation). Rounding the lips as in saying "Oh" is accompanied by sensations of tenseness in the lips. Retracting the tongue should call to your notice tensions in the tongue itself as well as in the region behind the chin, called the "floor" of the mouth.

If you have carried out the foregoing instructions, you are now prepared for practice on speech. After the customary five to fifteen minutes of preliminary relaxation, you are to count aloud to ten, sufficiently slowly so that you may observe what takes place. After a sufficient number of repetitions, you should perceive tension in your tongue, lips, jaw regions and throat, as well as vaguely in the diaphragm and all over the chest, as you produce each sound. If successful at these observations, you relax again for a while, then count half as loudly as before, when you should find that the same tensions recur but less strongly. Next you are to count similarly but so that you can scarcely be heard, making your observations. After further relaxation you are to count as before but this time not quite perceptibly, then less markedly than this and finally again less. According to reports, this becomes the same as when you imagine that you count from one to ten. The instruction now is to relax the speech apparatus completely—including the muscles of the tongue, lips, jaws, throat, chest and diaphragm. When you carry this out, you find that you no longer imagine in verbal terms—no longer speak to yourself.

Relaxing Speech Imagination

Thereupon you may imagine or recall yourself speaking in various ways, such as telling a waiter to bring your dinner or requesting a conductor to let you off the car. The good observer reports that he has slight tensions in the tongue, lips or throat as he speaks in imagination (sometimes also in the muscles of the jaw and floor of the mouth), and he does not fail to mention tensions in the chest and abdomen from breathing, which varies in its periods and pauses according to the character of the imagined speech. Imagining sounds also has been found to be accompanied by tensions, usually in the eye muscles, as if to look at the source of the sounds.

In high nerve tension the trained individual reports many gross and vague tensions in various parts of the body, sometimes fragmentary and elusive—abortive acts starting to do now one thing, now another—often without harmony or adequate coordination. So the highly nervous person describes his inner feelings, corresponding with our outward observations of his muscle tensions—his restlessness, shifting, grimaces, tics and other manifestations. We are led to the view that what you call the "feeling of nervousness" largely consists of the varied sensations from the disorderly muscular tensions, voluntary and involuntary, that mark your responses to environment.

It requires extreme progressive relaxation of the muscles of the eyes and speech apparatus to diminish mental activities. Considerable practice is necessary. You are simply to let these muscles go completely in the same manner as relaxing the muscles of the arm (Fig. 20).

Training in the measures described above enables you to observe what you are doing when you fail to sleep, as well as when you are mentally overactive or worried or are otherwise disturbed. Enabling you to make these observations starts you on the route toward doing away with undesirable overactivities. When you think or worry or are excited, you see things in imagination or say things to yourself. According to numerous observations, by finding what region is tense and relaxing it promptly you mechanically remove the disturbing activity.

Program for General Relaxation

After you have acquired a thorough understanding of what is meant by cultivating relaxation, it is recommended that you adopt a program of relaxing the various parts of the body. The following is a brief summary of such a program.

You are to assume a fairly comfortable position on a bed or wide couch, as described above, and then proceed as follows:

Right arm—practice one hour or more each day for about six days.

Left arm—continue to practice on the right arm and now at the same time also on the left arm one hour or more each day for about six days.

Right leg—continue to practice on both arms and now at the same time also on the right leg for nine days.

Left leg—continue to practice on all parts mentioned above and now at the same time also on the left leg for nine days.

Trunk—additional practice for three days.

Neck—additional practice for two days.
Forehead—one day.
Brow—one day.
Eyelids—one day.
Eyes—daily for one week.
Visual imagery—daily for one week.
Cheeks—one day.
Jaws—two days.
Lips—one day.
Tongue—two days.
Speech—three days.
Imagined speech—daily for one week.

Caution: Devote no more than the first portion of any period to learning to recognize tenseness in muscles, through the methods covered in the illustrations. The remaining time should be given over exclusively to complete relaxation. Never contract a part in order to relax it. *Avoid movements as an aid* during attempted relaxation; but also avoid holding still by a slight continuous tension, since this is not relaxing but only a useless imitation.

It is wrong for the beginner to claim that he does not feel the sensations where the arrows point. Whenever he moves normally he is guided by these sensations. They are felt, but he may not recognize them. The patient needs to learn to recognize when and where he tenses.

18

HOW TO RELAX
WHILE ACTIVE

"Learn to relax" originally meant to Mr. Doe merely that he should rest at frequent intervals. He did not see why he should need a doctor to aid him to carry out this prescription. When, during the early weeks of treatment, the doctor seriously undertook to teach him to let go muscle by muscle, while lying down, he wavered between uncertainty as to what it was all about and doubt that it was worthwhile. At times he was tempted to question the doctor's judgment and even sincerity. It was all so different from what he had come to regard as standard medical treatment for his condition—taking sedative medicines or listening to counsel and reassuring talk! At times he felt ill as well as discouraged; nevertheless the doctor continued impassively to teach him the next step, apparently understanding his complaints but evading his attempts to discuss them. There were other times when he felt better and ascribed his improvement to the treatment. Somewhat to his amazement the doctor greeted his enthusiasms no more cordially than his unfavorable opinions. He was encouraged only to maintain an open mind, to refrain from jumping at conclusions and to wait to pass judgment until he had learned to observe for himself. Above all, he was to practice regularly each day. On the whole, he was reminded of his experiences in school; he was receiving a course of instruction on how to behave when lying down. It differed from all the courses he had taken in school chiefly because the instructions were negative in effect. He was being taught merely *not* to do anything while attempting to rest. After all, it was very simple.

Although the doctor did not prophesy results, Mr. Doe, let us assume, believed that his sleep was becoming more restful at least on some nights, shortly before or after he had learned to relax his eyes fairly well; and at moments when he seemed to himself relaxed, he noticed for the time being a certain abatement of some of his former symptoms.

It seemed quite interesting when for the first time he was informed that today he was to sit up but that he should relax so far as possible in this posture. Because the muscles of his back and of certain other regions had to be tense in order to maintain the sitting position, while other muscles were relaxed, this was called "differential relaxation". He wished to ask various questions about differential relaxation, but instead the doctor encouraged him to observe for himself. Here, however, we need not hold back and so shall try to answer some of the questions Mr. Doe had in mind.

Perhaps his thoughts ran something like this: Before I took this course of treatment, I used to think of golf, billiards, the movies or some other form of recreation when I heard or read the word "relaxation". Now I have learned that for me at least the greatest relief from nervous strain comes when I lie down and let my muscles go completely in the manner I have been taught. It seems reasonable to assume that if I do this for an hour or two regularly each day, I should get somewhere in the course of time toward a calmer and quieter disposition. I am probably right in believing that I am sleeping better than before I began to take lessons. But I do not understand how anything more can be done or what is the purpose of my sitting up and being trained to relax in that position.

The doctor is accustomed to questions of this kind. Sometimes they come from persons (even a few doctors) who do not wish to consider evidence—being certain that learning to relax has nothing to do with overcoming nervous and other ills except insofar as the patient *believes* that benefit will result. With such persons, further discussion is perhaps better omitted. Consolation may be found in Aristotle's advice that one should limit one's arguments to those who are actually in doubt and who seek the truth rather than include those whose chief need is sharpened wits. Since John Doe belongs to the former class, the doctor reminds him how often in the past he has acted excitedly at a time when he might have carried out the same task in a calm manner. Such calmness under the circumstances would be called "differential relaxation". Or perhaps after some loss on the stock market or other misfortune, Mr. Doe tried to conceal his regrets but felt a strong inward emotion (which could have been detected by electrical tests). If he had greeted the loss with a reasonable degree of placidity, *inward* as well as *outward*, it would be an instance of differential relaxation.

To this John Doe replies, "I understand a little better what you mean, but can you give me more convincing illustrations?" Learning to dance, states the doctor, offers many illustrations. At first you moved stiffly and made unnecessary movements, then as you progressed you went through the same steps but let your limbs and trunk relax to a much greater extent. That was an instance of progressive differential relaxation.

To what has been said we may add that tests have been carried out on university students during such customary activities as reading and writing to see what happens under conditions favorable to relaxation. It was found that while they continued at the task their knee-jerks soon began to diminish, showing that their legs were relaxing. (The knee-jerk is the kick seen when a rubber-tipped hammer strikes the tendon below the knee-cap, provided that the thigh has been supported and that the leg and foot dangle freely.) The same tests on subjects previously trained to relax indicated that during periods when they were requested to relax these individuals showed a much more marked relaxation of the lower limbs while reading and writing than they did during periods when they were not so requested. These investigations afford evidence that some degree of relaxation frequently takes place during reading, writing and other customary activities in normal persons under favorable conditions and can be specially cultivated, if desired.

In a group of young women electrical measurements were made in the muscles which extend the leg. The legs hung freely while they read copies of a certain magazine. After about two months, during which they were instructed to relax their limbs in seven periods of treatment, the tests were repeated. Although instruction had been given only in the lying posture, a marked decrease in muscular tension was found as they sat reading the same magazine. Evidently they had become accustomed to be more relaxed, in their legs at least, under the conditions of reading. Other subjects, used as controls, who had received no training but who were tested similarly, showed no decline in tension, permitting the conclusion that the training had been effective. Such investigations lead us to believe that training can effect an economy of muscular energy during reading and other activities.

In various arts a type of relaxation has long been sought, although previous to the present studies it went unnamed. Teachers of speech and of singing, including the operatic type, devote much time to the relaxation of the muscles of the throat, larynx and respiratory organs. Singers early learn that a loud tone is not required in order to be heard in the back row of an auditorium with good acoustics. "Carrying power" of voice, as it is called, increases not alone with loudness but particularly also when the voice is properly placed. Even a whisper should be so uttered as to carry to the last row. It is commonly understood that voice placement depends largely upon proper relaxation. Generally the student is taught to locate his breathing expansion in the lower portion of the thorax (chest). When the lips, tongue and jaw are in the proper position for utterance, a minimum requisite of breath is expressed, chiefly from the lower part of the thorax. The student is particularly taught to sing with the throat and jaw muscles relaxed as much as possible. He is not to sing or speak "from the mouth", or carrying power will be lacking. Likewise, the timbre of the voice somewhat depends upon proper relaxation. The so-called throaty tone, which may mar a performance, is due to excess tension in throat and laryngeal muscles. Unfortunately, vocal teachers commonly lack an adequate knowledge of anatomy and physiology, which doubtless would greatly expedite their work.

In aesthetic and ballet dancing relaxation plays a conspicuous role. The individual who holds himself rigid in these arts fails in his effects. A particular exercise is repeated until grace is attained. This means that those muscles alone are used which are needed for the act and that no excess tension appears in them or in others. Delsarte undertook to prove that relaxation underlay the art of sculpture, indeed all the physical arts, and developed his so-called decomposing exercises in order to secure his aim. Certain philosophical works on aesthetics seem somewhat to realize these points, but they fall short of clear, well-defined statements.

There is evidence, then, that a person may be more or less excited—more or less tense—in various muscle groups during action. When a person acts with absence of excessive tenseness, we call his state "differential relaxation". *This term accordingly means the minimum of tensions in the muscles requisite for an act, along with the relaxation of other muscles.* A large variety of instances of differential relaxation can be found in daily life.

The speaker with a trained voice does not tire even after prolonged effort if he keeps his throat differentially relaxed. The billiard player spoils the delicate shot if he is generally too tense. The golf or tennis player learns to mingle a certain relaxation in strokes that are successful. The restless or emotional student finds it difficult to concentrate. The excited salesman fails to impress his prospective client. The clever acrobat produces an impression of grace and ease by relaxing such muscles as he does not require. The comedian often makes his ludicrous effects depend upon the extreme relaxation of certain parts of his body while others are active or held rigid. It seems safe to say that every learning process depends upon the acquisition of certain tensions with concomitant relaxations. Textbooks of psychology commonly illustrate the early learning process by the child at the piano, who squirms and shifts, perhaps even protrudes his tongue, when the notes are first studied. As skill is acquired, these tensions disappear; a certain degree of differential relaxation sets in.

With care you can observe excess tension in people around you every day. There are individuals who gesticulate unnecessarily, speak rapidly or with a shrill pitch, shift or turn about excessively, wrinkle their foreheads or frown too often, move their eyes unduly or show other signs of overactivity or excitement. Interesting imitations of high nervous tension in normal individuals under conditions of excitement can be found in almost every current exhibition of the motion pictures. Obviously, however, stagecraft is successful in its imitation of human activity in proportion as the total muscular patterns, including both tensions and relaxations, are duplicated.

In medical practice it has usually seemed simplest and most convenient to show the patient how to relax while lying down before training him in differential relaxation. For the treatment of chronic cases both types of training appear to be necessary, because the individual who remains excited during his daily activities does not readily relax when lying down. The tensions appear to be cumulative in their effects. For instance, according to modern experience the individual who has had insomnia for many years needs to be shown how to avoid not only restlessness at night but also undue excitement during the day. Conversely, the nervous, excitable individual needs to be shown not only how to be relaxed while at his activities but also how to avoid restlessness at night if sleep is to be made profound and restorative.

You are, therefore, to continue your daily practice lying down while you learn to form the new habit of being relaxed in the upright posture. A convenient way to begin is to relax thoroughly for fifteen to thirty minutes on a couch and then to shift slowly, with limply hanging limbs and head, to a nearby chair. You then relax all parts of your body in this new posture as well as you know how, keeping the eyes closed. You are to maintain sufficient stiffness of the back to prevent falling off the chair, but no more.

First Period

In the sitting posture a review of the same procedure as that followed while lying down is now initiated. Some nervous individuals at first desire the support of a pillow, but this is to be omitted as soon as possible. Keeping your eyes closed, bend your left arm; you should now be able to recognize distinctly the sensation of tenseness in the front part of the upper arm, even if no one helps you by holding the arm back and even if now you bend it only slightly (see Fig. 21). Having succeeded at this, let the left arm fall at your side, to rest fairly comfortably on some portion of the chair. The remainder of the first hour period of differential relaxation may be devoted to letting the left arm become as limp as possible and maintaining it so.

Second Period

On the following day you take the next step in a similar manner, extending your left forearm as in Fig. 4, but preferably without the use of books. If your forearm has been resting on the arm of your chair, bent at the elbow, move the wrist (with hand limp) so that the arm slowly becomes straightened. This permits you to observe the sensation in the rear of the upper arm when the triceps muscle contracts. Your practice most likely will be thorough if you devote the first portion of each hour period to recognizing the muscle sensation during a particular contraction and the remaining portion of the period to discontinuing this particular contraction. Day by day you are to repeat in a sitting position contractions of muscle groups in the same order as was followed in the previous chapter.

At this stage an experienced observer can readily tell if you are not well relaxed. If you are not, he notes that you sit with your head only partly bent over; the eyelids wink at times as in thinking or the limbs appear somewhat stiff. From time to time you may shift your position because of mild discomfort, but no such need arises, as a rule, during successful relaxation. If motionless but not well relaxed, you will probably discontinue your practice before an hour has elapsed, complaining of fatigue. The onset of fatigue during the attempt to relax clearly suggests that the directions given here are not being followed correctly.

Relaxing the Back and Neck

In preparing to relax the back, sit erect and note the sensation of tenseness along both sides of the spine. Having done so, you are to cease to be tense in these regions, letting go as far as you can without actually falling over or leaning uncomfortably far forward or backward. Upon coming to the muscles of the neck, you should note not only the tension in moving or inclining the head in any direction but also the slight static tension present when the head is held upright in ordinary posture. When the head droops during a prolonged period of relaxation in a sitting position, the subject generally complains at first of pain in some portion of the neck from ligaments that are being extended. This need not concern you, since adaptation usually sets in after a week or more of practice, and the pain diminishes or disappears.

Prior to experience with the method of relaxation, patients of a nervous type very often complain of a dull ache in the back of the neck or just above this region, in the head. Not infrequently the patient, after learning to recognize the experience of muscular contraction in the aching region, volunteers that the pain evidently arises from continued contraction there. Another type of ache or pressing distress due to chronic muscular contraction is called the "tension headache", which sometimes seems to be located at the top of the head. As the patient learns to relax the muscles of the forehead and brow, the pains may disappear—without suggestion from the physician that they will disappear and without his indicating what possibly has been their cause. You may have had similar experiences in the regions just mentioned or in others. But even if you learn to relax such regions and the distress disappears, you should be cautious in drawing conclusions as to what was the source of pain. Under similar circumstances the careful physician also is guarded in his reasoning.

It is particularly important to repeat the tensions of the eyes and the speech organs and to relax these anew in the sitting posture. According to the reports of many subjects, there occurs for a time a diminution of mental and emotional activity. Your purpose is to try to set up modified habits—"conditioning" yourself, as some call it—in the direction of greater nervous quiet when sitting up.

Relaxing Steady Tensions

Steady tensions may require special practice to relax. Even an experienced individual may continue to be somewhat rigid in a part which he believes to be quite relaxed. To learn to recognize the presence of tensions in such localities and to let them go step by step marks an important stage in learning to relax.

When the subject has become expert, his posture is typical (Fig. 22). The legs are more or less sprawled out and move limply if an observer pushes them. The arms and head droop flaccidly, and the trunk may be bent in any direction.

Breathing is regular and quiet. There is no trace of restless movement, even of a finger. A certain flattened or toneless appearance is characteristic of the eyelids, which do not wink during a prolonged period. This must be sharply distinguished from an earlier stage when the eyelids are held motionless for a time, followed by vigorous winking of the closed lids. Close observation should reveal no motion of the eyeball. To carry out these procedures properly, you will need the assistance of some person, who must learn to observe you carefully and to criticize you accordingly.

Relaxing the Eyes

If you have been successful up to this stage, you are now to learn to relax the eyes partially. You have previously learned to let the eyes go completely, so that they are not looking in any direction. But you cannot continue this with open eyelids for any considerable period because of a burning sensation due to the absence of winking and of adequate moistening of the eyeballs. Therefore, as a new practice, you are to permit the eyes to wander about to a slight degree, not letting them relax extremely. When this is done, a moderate amount of winking occurs, preventing discomfort and securing relative rest. Daily practice at complete relaxation of the eyeballs with closed lids and at partial relaxation with open lids may sooner or later lead you to feel that your eyes seem more rested; but such subjective impressions are not trustworthy unless sustained by findings of a careful oculist. We do not here seek to help you to "throw away your glasses", as is promised in certain books, which not only make unwarranted claims but also do not even advance correct methods to produce extreme ocular relaxation.

The above described methods of resting your eyes can be frequently applied at odd moments during the day. From time to time during prolonged reading it is probably good practice to rest them briefly in this way.

Relaxed Reading

Various periods of practice are devoted to reading. You are now to read, while relaxing the lower limbs; the back, so far as sitting posture permits; the chest, so far as can be done while inner speech continues; and the arms, so far as is possible while they hold the book or magazine. With the forehead and eyes extremely relaxed, you will of course not read. But you should relax these parts while holding the reading matter in order to become familiar with an extreme form of differential relaxation. A little more tension is then introduced; the words are to be read, but the eyes and other parts are to be kept as far relaxed as possible at the same time. Perhaps you find that you now follow the words but fail to get the meaning. This still represents too great a degree of relaxation. Accordingly, you are to read again, this time engaging in just enough contractions to get the meaning clearly but not more (Fig. 23).

These practices require the development of considerable skill, and the presence of an experienced critic is doubtless essential for the attainment of best results. But if the reader can succeed in securing even a slight measure of improvement in efficiency, he may perhaps consider his time well spent.

The effect of such practice, under medical direction (as tested by electrical measurements and certain other methods), is to tend to bring about a quieter state of body during reading, writing and other sedentary occupations (Fig. 24). According to reports, fatigue diminishes. Apparently restlessness, even if unnoticed, may interfere with attention and memory. This is perhaps because a generally tense state of muscles arouses sensations from these muscles which inhibit orderly thinking. Sometimes after relaxation has been learned, the patient asserts that he is able to work under noisy or otherwise irritating conditions, which formerly discomfited him. He may report less fatigue than formerly after working and perhaps also a generally increased efficiency. The accuracy of these reports has not yet been tested in the laboratory. My clinical impressions, which have little value as evidence but which serve to lead toward further investigations, are that in the course of weeks or months the individual's demeanor as well as countenance shows a change; his movements lose their quick, jerky habit; his voice becomes quieter and his speech slower; and lines of fear become less marked, as his anxious or worried appearance gives way to a more placid and restful expression.

When you read or write or are otherwise employed, certain activities evidently are an essential part of the process. These are called *primary* activities. Included among these are the contractions of those muscles needed for maintaining posture, for holding a book or pen, for moving the eyes to follow the print, and in most persons for moving the tongue and lips to repeat the words in inner speech. While all these primary activities join in the performance of a task, certain others may be observed in the average individual which apparently do not contribute but rather detract from his performance. These are called *secondary* activities, since they are not at all needed for the task in hand. Innumerable examples come to mind: While a person is reading, a noise in the next room may be followed by the individual's looking up and turning his head in that direction. Almost any distracting sound or sight may be followed by such secondary activity. Very often while reading or otherwise engaged the average individual is subject to an undercurrent of distracting thought processes in the form of worries, reflections, irrelevant recollections, intentions to do this or that thing; even songs or strains of music are silently but almost incessantly repeated. Many if not most persons read in this way, so that perfect attention to a book or occupation, even for so brief a time as a few minutes, is found perhaps only among those select individuals who have attained or are attaining eminent skill in their field.

Relaxation during activity should be applied to both primary and secondary activities. Primary activities may be unnecessarily intense for their purpose. For instance, a person may sing too loudly, pound his fist too vigorously as he converses, peer too intently, overexert himself in study. In such instances a better result will be produced by not trying so hard, by relaxation of primary activities. This relaxation should be carried only to the point where maximum efficiency continues; beyond this it would interfere with the purpose in hand. However, the aim is to carry relaxation of secondary activities to the extreme point, since these activities are generally useless.

We can briefly restate the substance of this chapter. In principle, vigorous activity is not precluded but rather is favored by a certain economy in the expenditure of neural and muscular energy. There is growing evidence that the average person whose organs are sound but who is nervously irritable and excited can learn to control these states by relaxing while he continues to engage in his daily affairs. As a result, it is now possible for many persons suffering from so-called nervous breakdowns to be spared the necessity of giving up their business, averting the additional worry and loss which they sustain when ordered to take the old-fashioned "rest cure" or to "leave town for a change".

Program for Differential Relaxation

After you have made yourself familiar with what is meant by relaxation during activities, it is recommended that you adopt a program of regular practice in relaxing the various parts of the body as far as possible while sitting up in a chair. Following is a brief summary of such a program.

Left arm—practice one hour or more each day for about six days.

Right arm and other parts—as related on pages 195 to 196, inclusive.

Sitting up, eyes open—relax eyes extremely till they burn; then close them. Repeat. One day of practice.

Sitting up, eyes open—relax eyes partially, permitting them to wander somewhat for two days of practice.

Reading—practice for two days or more.
Writing—practice for two days or more.
Conversing—practice for two days or more.

In addition to your practice one hour each day, try to keep in mind the aim to relax, as far as you can with undiminished efficiency, while engaged in your daily activities. See what you can do toward improving your game of golf through relaxation. By applying what you have learned, try to avert strain and fatigue in your arms and legs while driving your car. If you are a salesman, practice keeping your arms and legs relaxed while meeting customers. Perhaps you have discovered that there are certain muscles which you contract unnecessarily while at work and which you can relax instead.

19

INSTRUCTION BY THE DOCTOR OR EDUCATOR

Although this volume is addressed chiefly to healthy individuals and to persons who lack opportunity for medical consultation on matters of tension and relaxation, we pause now to ask how the doctor can aid and when and why he or another professional teacher is needed.

During the course of treatment by relaxation, as by any other method, symptoms of disease generally arise from time to time which require diagnosis, particularly in regard to whether they are appropriately treated by methods of relaxation. Obviously such questions require the attention of a competent physician, even if, prior to taking up relaxation, the patient has had a thorough physical examination.

But this is not all. The claims of any manual on relaxation must be modestly stated. As a rule, physical arts are not well learned from books alone but require personal instruction and example. To illustrate, a person may in some instances learn to play the piano or violin by himself, but his technique is likely to be inferior and therefore his accomplishments limited. This is particularly true in learning to relax. A physician is needed to point out to the patient when and where his tensions occur, to direct him where particularly to relax and to inform him whether he is succeeding or failing. (In determining this, electrical measurement is now a very important aid.) After training, the patient becomes better able to observe these matters for himself. But first old habits need to be overcome, and the patient commonly needs outside assistance to do this. Furthermore, he undertakes a difficult task when he starts to teach himself and is likely to become tense in certain respects in so doing. Skill in recognizing the experience of tension and its locality can be developed, I believe, if the directions given in this book are followed with care and patience. But not everyone will succeed in this independently, particularly under conditions of excitement or distress. In many instances of nervous disorder, judgment and self-control are impaired to such an extent that professional guidance is indispensable. While to most persons the sensation in a contracting muscle is a familiar experience, yet the fainter forms of this experience, so helpful in controlling relaxation, are most readily recognized with the aid of personal instruction.

Even the simple acts illustrated in the figures of Chapter 17 are seldom properly performed by most patients until after repeated instruction. For example, upon bending the right arm, they persist in holding the wrist stiff at the same time, thereby frustrating the attempt to effect contraction in one group of muscles as exclusively as possible. Again, when requested to cease contracting, many bring the hand back to the couch by contracting another set of muscles instead of simply letting go those muscles that were contracting. Correction of such errors obviously is most readily effected with the aid of the observing eye of an experienced physician. Many other such technicalities could be mentioned which hinder the progress of the patient unaided by personal instruction. There is also always the possibility that the individual, distracted as he is by other matters, will overlook his own tensions at particular moments and in impatience will give up the whole procedure.

While doubtless it is better than no rest at all, there is abundant evidence from clinical experience that the daily nap alone, so often recommended for the control of nervous and mental disorders, insomnia, colitis, high blood pressure and other serious conditions, has marked limitations. In many instances patients who for years have taken daily rests nevertheless come to the physician with conditions of high nerve tension or one of the other disorders mentioned. Indeed, even the patient who has been bed-ridden for years may be habitually overemotional and unrelaxed. Accordingly, it seems far from safe to assume that lying down each day in the hope of obtaining rest is equivalent to methodical treatment by relaxation (see page 164).

Teaching by the doctor (or educator) may differ in one important respect from learning to relax from this book. The doctor does not as a rule indicate to you in advance where you will observe the tenseness in each practice. Instead, you perform a given contraction and report where you believe that you have observed the signal which indicates tenseness to you. Learners often give wrong reports, whereupon the teacher can request them to contract again, without telling them where the tension is felt. It is best that the learner find it for himself without help from the doctor or other source. If the learner proves unsuccessful, the teacher eventually may tell him where to look.

Another impediment to self-instruction by the patient is the fact that he possesses no objective standard by which to judge his own improvement or deterioration. The opinion of the patient himself in this respect cannot be trusted. He is likely to be overenthusiastic or depressed at any particular time, and his views are likely to change. Past symptoms are likely to be forgotten or exaggerated in their intensity if he relies upon his own judgment and recollection. Scarcely more reliable are the opinions on his condition passed by members of his family and his friends. Testimonials are to be disregarded as more befitting advertisements of patent medicines or the claims of pseudoreligious cults than a scientific method carefully pursued. The doctor may show reasonable interest in the patient's reports on his own symptoms; but to be sure that improvement has really occurred, objective data are required, whether secured by electrical measurements, X-rays or other procedures suitable to the particular condition of the patient.

In his attempts to learn, the patient is aided by correction when he errs and by an "O.K." when he succeeds. Without such aid, I have found, he is often mistaken as to whether he has been successful and consequently may fall into wrong habits of tension or become unduly discouraged. This again is essentially what happens in learning anything; the teacher's comments are directive.

It is true that for success in overcoming high nerve tension the patient must progress through his own endeavors; but this does not mean, as some would believe, that science has nothing to offer him. Similarly, to learn mathematics or a foreign language, your own efforts are required and independence is ever to be encouraged; but this does not mean that teachers are useless. Rather, competent teaching takes advantage of knowledge and methods gained in the past so that the individual is enabled eventually to proceed by himself better than if he had been exclusively his own teacher.

This practical procedure is, of course, different from the methods of Coué and the pseudoreligious cults which teach the sufferer to say, "All is well", whatever the conditions. During treatment by relaxation reality is faced as such. The purpose is not to palliate the unavoidable hardships of life but to recognize them clearly and to live through them successfully. No attempt is made here to paint in joyful words what is plainly a source of misery. Rather, the aim is to reduce excess emotion so that adjustment can be made with such calm that health and efficiency are not seriously affected.

Patients who greet the physician as a great healer commonly make difficult pupils when learning to relax. They expect to lean on the doctor rather than to listen to his instructions and to follow them carefully. They are likely to ask him repeatedly for encouragement and for reassurance that their condition is not serious but is getting better. What is the doctor to do if he desires to avoid methods of encouragement and suggestion? The author's method has been to ask the patient to see if during such concern he is tense somewhere and, if so, to try to relax the tension. *It cannot be too much emphasized that the present method is limited to instructions to relax muscles and does not include attempts to effect results by suggestions and reassurances.*

Romance and imaginative appeal to patients are lacking in the method described here. Testimonial meetings, in which glasses and crutches are dramatically thrown away, do not occur. Improvement, when achieved, is a gradual growth and often is not accomplished so speedily as some patients demand. Often it is no more than wishful thinking to assume that one can get well fast. For those who need it most, there is no royal road to acquiring relaxed habits of living.

A difficult class of patients are those who, under treatment by the physician but not understanding the underlying principles, watch their symptoms from day to day or week to week in an endeavor to decide whether it is worthwhile to continue. When they feel better, they decide to go on; when they feel distressed or particularly fatigued, they are inclined to stop. Frequently such patients decide at a more advanced stage of treatment that their improvement has been sufficiently accomplished to make it unnecessary for them to continue. It then becomes the doctor's function to explain why their opinion is not to be relied upon.

A more intelligent patient attitude is illustrated in a subjective report from a physician who had been receiving treatment for overactive nerves along with symptoms of colitis. At the end of a six-month period, when he had been trained to relax lying down but not as yet sitting up, he stated that he no longer noted any of his previous symptoms but realized that it was for his physician to decide, on the basis of objective observations, when treatment should be terminated. Obviously, none but an experienced physician is qualified to decide at what stage of improvement treatment can be discontinued without danger of relapse.

Today a course of treatment most often requires one hour of instruction per month. However, the learner is furnished with printed cards informing him precisely what to practice on each day of the month. The instructions are simple, and no attempt is made to arouse confidence in the good effects to be expected from the treatment. Skepticism is no hindrance, provided that the patient practices faithfully, except in instances where skepticism evidently signifies preconceived ideas and indicates a lack of understanding of instructions. An important function of the physician is "police duty"—seeing to it that the patient practices regularly. Again, there are certain individuals who relax well upon request (as shown by electrical measurements) but who become excited under stress. These individuals require frequent reminders until differential relaxation becomes habitual.

Considerable variation exists in the length of time required for the treatment of different individuals, depending upon their age, previous habits, ability to follow directions, regularity of practice and of course upon the character and duration of their particular disorder. According to my experience, the individual of average intelligence, if regular at his appointments, can learn to relax, at least to a marked extent, fairly quickly. Children old enough to follow simple directions make apt pupils.

For relaxation treatment of speech difficulties in children six to ten years of age, the government of Canada's Department of Health and Welfare provided funds to the Rehabilitation Hospital of the University of Montreal under my supervision in the years 1962–1964. Satisfactory methods were developed.

Further developments for young children have been accomplished by Mike Marshall and Charles Beach of Michigan State University. Their specialty is "Method for Elementary School Incorporation of Tension Control into Their Curriculum".

The method of relaxation has proved suitable for treatment also of people of advanced age, provided that the patient's cooperation is obtained. Previous training in dancing, singing, piano playing, athletics, physical education and other activities in which muscular arts are cultivated shortens the time required to learn to relax completely. Needless to say, disorders that have persisted for years require longer periods of treatment than those that have endured for a relatively brief time.

In the previous chapters were described methods for doctors and their patients and for those laymen who are perhaps on the road to developing physical ills but who have not yet arrived. In the present chapter we have shown why in the management of certain disorders a doctor is indispensable for adequate results not only in diagnosis but also in cultivating relaxation. We have shown also that healthy children and adults can thrive under the teaching of educators and of clinical psychologists. They can learn to save their energy—their adenosine triphosphate.

We may conclude this chapter as follows: The present volume can be regarded as a beginner's manual of progressive relaxation for use alone or preferably under instruction by a physician or educator experienced in the technique.

Even if used alone, it is designed to be a useful aid during rest and during active life. We can reasonably expect that with daily practice the results will often include at least moderate saving of energy expenditure and at least moderate reduction of fatigue, insomnia, digestive and other tension disorders.

On the other hand, the use of this manual alone is not expected to effect marked lasting reduction of essential hypertension. This attainment can be expected to require a medically trained instructor. Similar requirements are to be anticipated for the successful treatment of severe anxiety states and other severe medical conditions. The more moderate the expectations, the greater likelihood of pleasing results.

20

MEASURING
PERSONAL ENERGY
EXPENDITURES

Science is not born suddenly, like Venus emerging from the ocean. Still unknown to many, we have *gradually* attained a science of nerve and muscle tension, but this has been preceded by centuries of misleading speculations and theories, which tend to become fixed even in some scientists.

Let me tell the story briefly. Less than a century ago a well-known American doctor wove a theory that nerves often became "weak". He named this hypothetical condition "neurasthenia", and this term came into general diagnosis among doctors of the last century and survived into the present one. He wrote a book entitled *Fat and Blood and How to Make Them*, advising doctors to order their nervous patients to prolonged bed rest and, as a *cure*, to have them eat as many as a dozen eggs per day. This overfeeding treatment in bed was the *rest cure* of Dr. Weir Mitchell. Many doctors and even some scientists falsely assumed that what he prescribed was chiefly rest in his "rest cure". What he really advocated was a special *copious diet* during bed rest. Quite unknown in his day was high nerve and muscle tension. Quite unknown likewise was the need of the populace for progressive relaxation. Patients were not yet advised to relax. As I have related elsewhere, even in the decade of President Wilson, relaxation was not yet discovered by the medical profession, for in his doctor's book on *rest*, the word "relaxation" does not appear even in the index.

Returning to the history of Dr. Weir Mitchell, he and his followers failed to advance evidence for his theory that nerves become "weak" and that the cure is diet during rest. Today his theory is in the discard.

Accordingly, it is striking that many people who have never even read his book credit Dr. Weir Mitchell with something he could never have rightly claimed and of which he never wrote—namely, knowledge of relaxation of muscle and nerve.

He did not emphasize what we have termed habitual nerve and muscle relaxation, nor did he contrast this with habitual excessive tension.

Not only did he not use the word "relax"; he was not interested in the muscle system and evidently lacked knowledge about it, never mentioning that this comprises 40 to 50 percent of the body weight. There is no evidence that he knew the number of skeletal muscles in the body.

Nevertheless, Dr. Weir Mitchell is considered by many, including the present author, to have been the greatest neurologist of his day. He was too honest a man to desire false credit for knowledge of the field about which this book is written.

Another theory, which became entrenched in the 1890s and which at present is losing adherents, rests on the belief that we do not know why we act as we do when nervous; the cause of neurotic conditions, they say, is like the iceberg, of which but a small part is visible above the surface of the sea, much the greater bulk lying submerged. To discover the cause some analyst must delve into the secrets of our dreams and explore the hidden meanings of our acts. Adherents of this doctrine invariably trace the source of nervousness to matters of sex—particularly the sort of sex life and development which they believe that we had unconsciously during early infancy.

The average physician in this country is kept too busy with visible matters of fact to have time to spare for fine-spun or fantastic theories concerning nervousness. Since an examination of the nerves and brain of nervous people, living or dead, as a rule discloses no tumor, no inflammation, no injury and no other alteration of structure which the skilled eye can detect, he has had until recently no tangible facts with which to work. But, lacking such facts and finding little appeal in speculative philosophies of any kind, many doctors have suspected that nervousness generally is secondary to other diseases or else is a sort of imaginary nothing. As one doctor recently commented, "It is only a state of mind".

Opposing the view that nervousness is merely an effect of other diseases are various well-known facts: that many children who are otherwise healthy are highly nervous; that adults differ widely as to how they meet the same disease conditions—some excitedly, others quite calmly; that the discovery and removal of a diseased tissue (such as a region of inflammation or tumor) in an excitable person commonly do not alter his nervous habits permanently; that in everyday life many events obviously give rise to highly excitable states of mind without any disease being involved. Such events are automobile and other accidents, including fires, where no personal injury occurs, illness or death of dear ones, loss of position or station or loss of fortune.

Amid the welter of conflicting theories concerning nervousness, attempts to get at the facts by established scientific procedures have been conspicuous by their absence. In this, as in other subjects, we should expect the genuine beginning of scientific progress to be marked not by the spinning of theories but by the precise and orderly description of phenomena, followed as soon as possible by accurate measurement. Hoping to get somewhere by these methods, some seventy years ago I began a study of the start or jerk which some persons, nervous or otherwise, sometimes evince following a sudden noise or other strong excitation, usually while they are otherwise engaged. As is well known, extremely nervous persons often start on such occasions and sometimes report that they have had sensations of "shock". By means of a relatively crude device attached below the back of the neck, it was possible at that time very roughly to measure movements of the trunk. Tests in this manner readily confirmed the popular conception that persons showing other symptoms of nervous excitement often jerk violently when a sudden noise is made, particularly if they have been deeply engrossed in other matters.

Likewise, if the subjects, while sitting, were requested to hold the muscles of the limbs, head and trunk stiff, they generally started violently. This occurred not only with those who seemed highly nervous but with others as well. When, on the other hand, the subjects relaxed their muscles as completely as they knew how, the start was generally diminished; the subjects reported that there was little or no shock and the sound seemed to lose its irritating character.

So many muscles jerk during the nervous start

that it has not yet proved possible to record the agitation suitably by mechanical means. Therefore, in 1924 Miss Margaret Miller, a graduate student, and I turned to a simpler act for study. The subject lay upon a couch with eyes closed, his right arm outstretched so that the fingertips made contact with a little salt solution, through which we could pass, when we wished, a momentary but painful electric current. We were able to control the current in duration and other essential characteristics so as to keep it constant for each subject throughout all the tests. Each time the subject felt the painful shock he withdrew his hand in haste. Since his upper arm was fastened down, he could withdraw the hand only by bending his forearm. We recorded the speed and extent of this movement.

In one set of tests the subject lay quietly, with eyes closed, resting as persons ordinarily rest. In another set of tests, alternating with the first set, he was requested to relax extremely according to the methods I have described, in which he had been trained for several months previously. For almost all of the subjects the results were strikingly different in the two sets of tests: Following the instruction to relax extremely, the speed and extent of the jerk as a rule were greatly diminished. One subject, who relaxed most extremely as judged by other signs, did not withdraw her hand at all as a rule in an entire series of tests. Afterward she was amazed to learn that the strength of the shocking current was the same when she was extremely relaxed as when she was resting less quietly.

Such findings lead to interesting considerations. Individuals who start at sudden "shocks" naïvely try to explain their agitation as due to something outside of themselves—namely, the strong character of the disturbance. However, according to our tests, a violent reaction along with subjective distress seems to depend not only upon the exterior disturbance but also upon the preceding state of the muscles of the subject. Some individuals do not as a rule start visibly, but all withdraw their hands if the shock is sufficiently strong, provided that their muscles have been held moderately tense. On the other hand, as stated above, when the individual was extremely relaxed, the feeling of "nervous shock" was weak or absent, and the start, or withdrawal, was either absent or slight. These observations suggested the possibility that *all* subjective irritation or distress might be reduced if the individual were to become sufficiently relaxed; this hypothesis remains today a beacon light for further experiments and observations. A psychologist working in another laboratory has confirmed our finding that advanced relaxation tends to diminish certain types of pain.

The start is particularly marked in so-called irritable or excitable or nervous persons. It tends to be marked not alone in neuroses but also, as is well known, after operations and various forms of prolonged illness. Nervous individuals are not only easily disturbed by noises which tend to interrupt their train of thought, but they are distracted by many other types of stimuli (not necessarily sudden or unexpected) which do not affect phlegmatic individuals to the same degree. Events of little importance and pains from slight tissue changes are particularly likely to arouse distress in such individuals to the point of interrupting their useful pursuits. In fact, their subjective symptoms of distress appear to mount as they become increasingly irritated and excited. It seems probable that the physiology underlying this is a heightened nerve-muscle tension, which would readily account for many characteristics of individuals in a "nervous" state.

Perhaps the most commonly used test for nervousness is the knee-jerk, elicited by striking the tendon below the kneecap, while the thigh rests on a support so that the foot swings freely. The attention of the subject must be turned to other matters when the tap comes, or he is likely to hold the leg stiff, preventing the kick. Under these conditions if he is generally excited or if his muscles generally are in a state of moderate contraction, the kick is marked. But during extreme relaxation either in subjects previously trained to relax or in those who relax extremely without training, the kick is diminished or absent, as shown by Anton J. Carlson and the author in various tests.

By use of the methods described above, a certain movement may be repeatedly aroused in the subjects. In each case a disturbance in the sense organs is propagated through nerves to the central nervous system and then instantly back through other nerves to muscles, which thereupon are caused to contract. Such action is called "reflex". Arousing reflexes affords valuable information in the study of nervousness but is limited as a method of scientific investigation and leaves us without any standard of adequate measurement.

The problem faced in the author's studies some years ago was that persons might lie or sit outwardly quiet or almost so and yet show various clinical evidences of being nervously disturbed. Was it possible, for example, that an arm which appeared motionless to the naked eye nevertheless contained muscles engaged in slight but active contraction?

The beginnings of an instrumental approach to this problem had been laid by a very early investigator in animal electricity. In 1842 Carlo Matteucci, working on frogs' muscles, discovered that if he pinched a muscle or otherwise caused it to contract, he could detect at the moment of the contraction a faint wave of electrical current. Since that time workers in noted physiological laboratories all over the world have confirmed his discovery, making it seem probable that marked contraction of muscle can always be detected with electrical apparatus suitably sensitive. In 1907 another investigator in a German laboratory, H. Piper, first studied muscle contractions in man. His method was to have his subjects bend their right arm relatively quickly. My hope that the then newly developed vacuum tube would aid in these studies was particularly encouraged when, in 1921, Alexander Forbes and Catherine Thatcher, two investigators at Harvard University, first employed such tubes in the study of human muscle activities. During subsequent years, amplifiers have come to be widely used in the study of nerves and muscles. But the various equipment developed in 1927 evidently was not sufficiently sensitive to test whether or not a muscle, apparently in repose, was really giving off slight electrical currents, which would indicate a state of active contraction. I found it necessary to construct an assembly capable of measuring accurately such faint quantities as one millionth of a volt. In this task the Bell Telephone Laboratories very generously cooperated as a public service.

In making observations of the electrical impulses present in muscles during contraction, it was formerly necessary for accuracy to insert pins (of platinum iridium) into the muscles of the patient. Now these are omitted. Instead, I employ surface electrodes of certain dimensions.

I named the instrument thus designed jointly with the Bell Telephone Laboratory technicians the "integrating neurovoltmeter". Early models were employed in my laboratory in the Department of Physiology at the University of Chicago until 1936, later models since then in my Laboratory for Clinical Physiology in downtown Chicago. During the past forty years the instrument has been used on most days in human measurements. In 1975 we perfected a small portable model for use by others.

With the aid of the integrating neurovoltmeter and other instruments we are continuing daily to make new, basic measurements bearing on medicine and the life sciences. Included among our subjects are not only patients with tension and allied disorders, such as essential hypertension and spastic digestive tract, but also individuals selected at random from the populace who state that they have no complaints and who are apparently healthy. Thus we are beginning to accumulate a wide variety of statistics concerning what might be called the economics of the systems of the human body. We record neuromuscular and other bodily performances averaged per minute in relation to the energy expenditures measured and averaged during the same unit of time.

For examples, during each thirty-minute period of test, among the determinations averaged per minute are cardiac output and peripheral resistance as well as systolic and diastolic pressures, chemical values of muscular energy costs and measurements of various other physiological functions. For each minute, our digital computer simultaneously records each of the many energy functions averaged per minute. Following the thirty minutes of measurements, it automatically typewrites a tabular account of the many values averaged per minute.

Thus a wealth of data is being added to our scientific and clinical knowledge about human muscle action and contraction and about nerve impulses and nervous states. This knowledge, along with other publications, is the basis of the present popularly addressed volume, including description of the scientific application of progressive relaxation and of self-operations control.

21

RELAXING THE MIND

Even before World War I, a French physician, Dr. Laroussinié, called attention to the increase of nervous disorders in all countries. The psychopathic hospitals, public and private, were becoming insufficient to satisfy the demands made on them. He found the cause for these widespread nervous disorders in the "state of mind" that characterized the civil population: in the chasing after immediate wealth and material possessions which replaced the patient toil of our forefathers; in addiction to dances, alcohol and fast automobiles. These causes combined to raise new generations lacking in balance and self-control, impulsive and dangerous to society and to the state.

In a high-spirited people, like the American, ever on the alert toward new developments—financial, scientific, educational, artistic and social—we should naturally expect to find many overactive minds. Such advanced attainments generally come only after much thinking, and the rich and varied rewards offered in a lusty growing nation provide continual stimulation. The difficulties of the times and the efforts on all sides to reconstruct our economic system have, so to speak, only added fuel to our mental fires. Now we find ourselves facing an uncertain future which will require our clearest thinking and our fullest efforts if our liberties are to survive.

In a period marked by epochal changes, the life of each individual is necessarily affected. Adjustments to a more or less altered social order prove disturbing, adding to the problems which have to be met and tending toward the increase of high nerve tension. Under these conditions it seems safe to assume that almost any active individual has at times found himself obsessed by reflections and worries which he seemed unable to throw off. Various factors in modern life tending to incite excessive thinking and emotion have been sufficiently mentioned in earlier chapters. We are led to ask what can be done, if anything, to effect mental quiet amid all this turmoil.

Something like this question was on the tip of John Doe's tongue before he got very far in learning to relax. He began to recognize that

possibly his bodily complaints such as his vague
pains which he sometimes felt near the heart, the
skipped beat, the discomfort in his abdomen due
to what he called "gas" might be due to his
muscular tensions, and he did not doubt that he
would feel better in many ways if he really
learned to relax. However, he realized that he
worried too much and he considered this a trouble
of his mind, not his body. At times he wondered
whether he ought to go to work at all and occasionally he felt like dodging rather than meeting
people. Often he did not seem able to concentrate
as of old and his memory seemed impaired. More
frequently than seemed good for him, he felt
emotionally upset and sometimes even began to
fear that he might pass into a state of panic.

He had read in many books that mental troubles commonly arise from failure to express your
emotions. Maybe, he reflected, a fuller emotional
expression was what he needed. He did not see
that this would be provided however well he
might learn to relax.

It is no wonder that John Doe had these
misgivings. All of his life he had been accustomed
to distinguish between his mind and his body.
When he worried, he believed that he did so
with his mind, not with his body. No doubt, he assumed, worry occurred as an act of the brain. To
this extent, worry was something, he reflected, that
went on in the body but it was within a particular
part of the body—namely, the skull. What was

true of worry, he believed, was likewise true of his memory and his attention, his fears and other emotions and especially his imagination. He yielded to the belief that mental activities occur in the mind and when muscles become tense, this is only a result or expression of what goes on in the mind. He maintained, therefore, that while relaxing might do him a lot of good, it could hardly be expected to take care of his mental ills. To this he added a further objection and difficulty. He found that when he was emotionally upset he failed to relax. From this he concluded that he lacked the will power to relax. From this objection he passed on to another—namely, that he could not be expected to relax in the presence of so much distress unless something was first done to improve his mental state.

John Doe came by his views honestly. He inherited them from his forefathers, including those of the nineteenth century. As he learned to observe accurately what took place at moments when he worried, imagined, recalled or engaged in some other particular mental activity, he became enlightened. He acquired a new conception of what actually goes on during moments of worry and other mental activity. Experience taught him that the mind was not what he had believed it to be, following tradition. He acquired a new working conception, and with the aid of a little explanation he no longer assumed that whenever he worried it was an act of his brain alone. For one thing, he learned that as he relaxed, he ceased to worry! This surprised him!

Three score years ago evidence that individuals could be trained to relax to the point of diminution or disappearance of worrying and other emotional overactivity would doubtless have received scant consideration. Most neurologists as a rule were not interested in the scientific study of mental processes. We then lived in an era of nervous medicine (not yet wholly past) which was skeptical rather than creative and therefore resistive rather than constructive. Its skepticism, moreover, was generally founded not on careful studies showing negative results but on pseudo-authoritative dogmatism. Some physicians of the old school would have said that all instructions such as given here are mere "suggestions" to the patient and that the results are wholly due to his believing them. According to these physicians, wiggling a patient's right toe or giving him a bread pill would produce the same favorable result as relaxation and by the same means if the patient believed it would. They would have felt certain, without investigation, that lying down daily for an hour to relax without instruction would accomplish the same results as relaxing with instruction, provided that the patient believed it would.

Their view has not withstood the test of time, for I have shown that in many cases technical relaxation can succeed where daily rest alone has failed.

The method of laboratory investigation teaches us to refrain from jumping to conclusions and makes it readily possible to arrange conditions from which the effects of "mental suggestion" can be excluded. Does muscular relaxation bear any relation to thinking, emotion and other so-called mental activities?

Investigations bearing on this problem were begun at the University of Chicago in 1922 and were continued there until 1936. Since then they have been conducted at my Laboratory for Clinical Physiology. Clinical records had been made previously in great detail. For scientific study it was of course necessary to consider only very simple types of mental activity, such as could readily be aroused in the laboratory when desired. The subjects had been trained to relax, as well as to report on their subjective experiences from muscular contractions.

Since the time of Francis Galton (1888) it has been known that all persons necessarily employ some images in their various forms of thinking, emotion and other mental activity. If you imagine a building or any other concrete object, you will probably see some sort of picture of it; this picture is relatively clear in some persons but in others is likely to be fragmentary, vague and fleeting. Some persons experienced in the scientific examination of their sensations report that they have few or no such visual images. Again, if they imagine or recall some sound, whether noisy or musical, most persons state that they seem to hear something more or less clear and perhaps have a vague sensation in the ear. When you imagine or recall tasting or smelling, reproductions in kind are likely to occur. Trained observers have generally agreed also that when they imagine or recall some muscular act they have an experience which seems faintly to reproduce or to resemble what takes place during the actual performance. Other sensations and feelings are often reproduced in us in much the same way. According to reports by experts, while individuals differ greatly in the ability and extent to which they employ these various types of imagery, it is agreed that everyone makes use of some types of images whenever he thinks. This point would be admitted even by certain students who hold that at certain significant moments our thinking is without images.

Accordingly, the subjects in our investigations, lying on couches under conditions favorable to relaxation, were at proper moments requested to imagine or to recall various simple matters and to describe what takes place at such moments. No subject was informed as to what the other reported; yet, following repeated observations, they practically all agreed that when they saw pictures in imagination or recollection, they simultaneously had faint sensations as if their eye muscles were contracting to look in the direction of the pictured object. Upon relaxing the eye muscles completely, they reported that the visual images subsided or disappeared. When requested to imagine counting to ten or to recall the words of a poem or something they had recently said, most of them stated that they had sensations in their tongue and lips and throat as if they were actually speaking aloud, except that they were much fainter and briefer. Upon relaxing the tongue, lips and throat muscles completely, most of them stated that imagining or recalling the numbers or words was discontinued. Some of the subjects believed that with relaxation of the organs of speech they still *visualized* numbers or words, but they agreed that sensations from the eye muscles seemed present at such moments. Following the instruction to relax completely the muscles of the eyes and of speech, all the subjects agreed that mental activity subsides or disappears. The investigator was careful to avoid suggesting his views to any subject. It was apparent in each instance that the observations were firsthand.

While the account given above is admittedly sketchy and incomplete, it will serve here to give a general idea of the manner and direction of our early investigations. Readers interested in a more precise account will find this in *Progressive Relaxation.* See page 254.

What subjects report about their experiences, however technically they are trained to observe, is open to possible test if we have suitably sensitive instruments that can be appropriately applied. The possibility of detecting and measuring what takes place in the body at a moment of mental activity was the incentive that led to the development of the electrical apparatus previously described.

Here is an illustration. The subject lies relaxed upon the couch with eyes closed. He is instructed to engage in a particular mental activity at the first click of a telegraph key and to relax any muscular tensions present at a second signal. The wires attached to the electrical recording apparatus are connected with electrodes on the skin over the muscles that bend the right arm.

As previously stated, when a trained subject is instructed to remain relaxed, the needle on the dial remains quiet. But when, for instance, the instruction is to imagine lifting a weight with the right forearm, the first signal is promptly followed by a series of long vibrations of the needle, which cease soon after the signal to relax. However, when the instruction is "Imagine lifting with the left arm" or "Imagine bending the left foot", no electrical changes are recorded from the right arm, and the needle remains quiet as during complete relaxation. It remains quiet during various other kinds of such critical tests, which are called control tests.

If the subject has been requested to imagine striking a nail twice with a hammer in his right hand, two series of vibrations generally occur with a short intervening interval of quiet needle. Beautiful registration is secured following instruction to imagine or recall some rhythmical act, such as shaking the furnace.

To register what takes place during visual imagery, the surface electrodes from which wires lead to the integrating neurovoltmeter are placed above and below one eye or to the right and left of one eye. When the eyes turn in a particular direction—for instance, up—a distinctive pattern is recorded on the graph. Upon instructing the subject to imagine particular visual objects, characteristic patterns are also recorded in most instances. For example, the pattern upon imagining the Eiffel Tower is the same as that for looking up. The conclusion seems justified that when you see visual pictures in imagination or recollection your eye muscles actually contract—however slightly—just as they do to a larger degree when you actually see; that is, you actually look in the direction of the imagined object. Furthermore, just as you exercise control on what you see by directing your gaze this way or that, you likewise control your imagination and course of thinking, at least with respect to the visual elements.

In certain studies the electrodes relate to the tongue, lips or region of the vocal cords to test muscles of speech during various types of thinking. If the subject imagines counting or recalls the words of a poem or song, a specialized pattern is in each instance immediately recorded. Even when he thinks of certain abstract matters, such as the meaning of the term "infinity", there is evidence in many instances that his vocal organs move in a slight and abbreviated manner as if they were actually saying words.

Accordingly in the early 1930s I showed that our mental activities, in addition to images and perhaps other elements, essentially involve faint and abbreviated muscular acts. These findings have been confirmed by other investigators. There has been abundant evidence in these as well as in many other of our clinical studies that with the relaxation of such muscular acts, the entire process of thinking practically ceases as long as the relaxed state persists.

When a patient worries or engages in other disturbing mental activities, we may profitably ask him, if he has been adequately trained to report, what takes place at such moments. He states as a rule that he has visual and other images concerning the matter troubling him and slight sensations, as from eye-muscle and other muscle tensions, while he sees and otherwise represents to himself what the trouble is about. We have grounds for assuming that such reports in general probably are substantially true, since electrical methods have confirmed the presence of muscular contractions during such mental activities as have been tested up to 1976. During extreme worry, fear or general emotional upset, the investigator who attaches his electrodes relative to any nerve or muscle will generally find the part in a varying state of high tension (technically speaking, marked action potentials can be detected).

Since the reports mentioned have been confirmed, two ways seem open in clinical practice toward ridding the patient of worry and other disturbing mental activity. One is to train him to relax generally; the other is to train him to relax specifically the tensions involved in the particular mental act of worry or other disturbance. In general relaxation a stage is reached when, as can be noticed, the eyeballs cease looking, the closed lids appear flabby and free from winking, the entire region of the lips, cheeks and jaws seems limp and motionless and breathing shows no irregularity. Interrupted after such an experience, the trained patient reports that for the time being he was free from mental disturbance, since all imagery had indeed ceased. Such reports have been secured from a number of patients who were not told in advance what to expect; to some the results came as a surprise, since they had previously failed to see how relaxing muscles alone could have any bearing upon their mental problems. Since we find that maintaining general relaxation succeeds in markedly reducing, perhaps to zero, disturbed mental states, it seems reasonable to expect that with repetition and practice relief can be made more nearly permanent. This attempt has been described by Professor Anton J. Carlson as the reverse of the method of habit formation studied by Pavlov and his associates in Russia. While their work consists in forming new habits, here the attempt is to undo old connections.

Accordingly, to train the patient to free himself from a particular form of anxiety or other disturbance requires that he first learn to observe and report accurately his sensations. He is then to practice relaxing the muscular tensions characterizing a disturbed state at the same time that he goes about his daily affairs. This is, again, differential relaxation. For example, a person may find himself continually recalling events in which he lost financially, thus disturbing his present efforts to work. If such disturbing reflections are found to include visual pictures of those events along with sensations as from eye muscles tensed to look at the pictures, the instruction is to relax such tensions while not closing the eyes and not otherwise ceasing to be active.

We see again the answer to the question, What have muscle tensions to do with worry, fear and other states of mind? Tests indicate that when you imagine or recall or reflect about anything, you tense muscles somewhere, as if you were actually looking or speaking or doing something, but to a much slighter degree. If you relax *these particular tensions*, you cease to imagine or recall or reflect about the matter in question—for instance, a matter of worry. *Such relaxations may be accomplished no less successfully while you are active in your daily affairs than while you are lying down.*

Our studies concerning the electrophysiology of mental activities have been confirmed in many laboratories. Our principles and methods of progressive relaxation relating to education and to experimental and clinical psychology are currently taught in most American universities and colleges.

It is important to realize that the participation of muscular tension patterns in mental activities at every moment was shown by our own graphs and measurements in the 1930s, with almost daily confirmation in our laboratory since then and with confirmation by various other investigators. *Thus the peripheral nature of every mental activity is established* no less than the participation of the brain and the nature of mental activities is no longer a matter of theory.

In other words, my measurements disclosed that the "mind" is the function of the brain plus the neuromuscular system. It is the activity of a section of the body, just as the digestive and circulatory systems are the activity of two other sections. Thus the nature of the mind is no longer a philosophical enigma. Science has replaced speculation.

Since today many psychologists employ this book for teaching and other purposes, the following paragraph is addressed specifically to these scientists and teachers. To avoid misinterpretation, I wish to emphasize that to my knowledge my investigations have never produced evidence favoring what they call "the motor theory of consciousness". By this they mean that impulses passing in nerves to the brain, which stimulate activities in the brain, become conscious only at the moment they are followed by impulses which proceed from the brain to muscles. I know of no scientific way to test this theory and never have regarded it with interest. On the contrary, it has seemed to me highly speculative. My early investigations established the importance of sensations from the joints, tendons and other bodily tissues, which psychologists call "propioceptive sensations". No one doubts that images and other representations called "associations" play a part in our mental activities. I assume that consciousness in man inextricably includes impulses to the brain, in the brain and from the brain retroactively back and forth. Therefore, I deplore that in various textbooks of psychology my measurements of mental activities have been regarded as evidence for "the motor theory of consciousness", which I have opposed as speculative and unphysiological since 1907, when I became a graduate student at Harvard in the department of Hugo Munsterberg, who advocated the motor theory of consciousness and of which I was openly unconvinced.

Books by Dr. Jacobson

Progressive Relaxation	University of Chicago Press 5801 South Ellis Chicago, Illinois 60637
You Must Relax	McGraw-Hill Book Company 1221 Avenue of the Americas New York, New York 10020
How to Relax and Have Your Baby	McGraw-Hill Book Company
Tension Control for Businessmen	The National Foundation for Progressive Relaxation 55 East Washington Chicago, Illinois 60602

Anxiety and Tension Control	J. B. Lippincott 5 East Washington Square Philadelphia, Pennsylvania 19105
Tension in Medicine	Charles C. Thomas (Edmund Jacobson, Editor) 301–327 East Lawrence Street Springfield, Illinois 62717
Biology of Emotions	Charles C. Thomas
Modern Treatment of Tense Patients	Charles C. Thomas
Teaching and Learning	The National Foundation for Progressive Relaxation
How to Teach Scientific Relaxation	The National Foundation for Progressive Relaxation
Principles of Psychiatry and Clinical Psychology	To Be Completed in 1976
You Can Sleep Well	McGraw-Hill Book Company (out of print)

Volumes of Articles by Dr. Jacobson

Volume 1: *Direct Electrical Measurement of Mental Activities in Action Potentials*

Volume 2: *Essential Hypertension and Coronary Disease*

Volume 3: *Activity and Relaxation in Muscle and Nerve in Intact Man—Detection and Measurement*

Volume 4: *Publications in Philosophy, Psychology and Medicine*

These volumes are published by The National Foundation for Progressive Relaxation

Publications by Dr. Jacobson

1910   "The Relational Account of Truth," *J. Philos., & Sci. Method*, 7:253–261, May 1910.

1910   "Inhibition," doctoral thesis, Harvard University, 1910.

1911   "On Meaning and Understanding," *Am. J. Psychol.*, 22:553–577, October 1911.

1911   "Experiments on the Inhibition of Sensations," *Psychol. Rev.*, 18:24–53, January 1911.

1911   "Consciousness under Anaesthetics," *Am. J. Psychol.*, 22:333–345, July 1911.

1912   "Further Experiments on the Inhibition of Sensations," *Am. J. Psychol.*, 23:345–369, July 1912.

1917   "The Reduction of Gastric Acidity, *J. AMA*," 69:1767–1768.

1920   "Use of Relaxation in Hypertensive States," *N.Y. Med. J.*, March 6, 1920.

1920   "Reduction of Nervous Irritability and Excitement

by Progressive Relaxation," *Trans. Sec. Nervous & Mental Diseases, AMA*, 1920.

1921　"Treatment of Nervous Irritability and Excitement," *Illinois Med. J.*, March 1921.

1921　"The Use of Experimental Psychology in the Practice of Medicine," *J. AMA*, 77:342–347.

1922　"Christian Science from a Medical Standpoint," *Ill. Med. J.*, December 1922.

1924　"The Technic of Progressive Relaxation," *J. Nervous & Mental Disease*, 60 (6):568–578, December 1924.

1924　"The Physiology of Globus Hystericus," *J. AMA*, 83:911–913, September 1924.

1925　"Progressive Relaxation," *Am. J. Psychol.*, 36:73–87, January 1925.

1925　"Voluntary Relaxation of the Esophagus," *Am. J. Physiol.*, 72 (3):387–394, May 1925.

1925　Jacobson, E., and A. J. Carlson, "The Influence of Relaxation upon the Knee-jerk," *Am. J. Physiol.*, 73 (2):324–328, July 1925.

1926　"Response to a Sudden Unexpected Stimulus," *J. Exp. Psychol.*, 9 (1):19–25, February 1926.

1926　"Spastic Esophagus and Mucous Colitis," *Trans. Sec. on Gastroentrol and Proctocol of the AMA*, 1926.

1927　"Spastic Esophagus and Mucous Colitis," *Arch. Internal Med.*, 39:433–435, March 1927.

1927　"Action Currents from Muscular Contractions During Conscious Processes," *Science*, 66 (1713):403, October 28, 1927.

1928　"Quantitative Recording of the Knee-jerk by Angular Measurement," *Am. J. Physiol.*, 86 (1):15–19, August 1928.

1928　"Newer Studies of Relaxation and Sleep," *Univ. Chicago Mag.*, 21 (1):22–25, November 1928.

1928　"Differential Relaxation During Reading, Writing

and Other Activities as Tested by the Knee-jerk," *Am. J. Physiol.*, 86 (3):675–693, October 1928.

1930 "Electrical Measurements of Neuromuscular States during Mental Activities"

1930   1. "Imagination of Movement Involving Skeletal Muscle," *Am. J. Physiol.*, 91 (2):567–608, January 1930.

1930   2. "Imagination and Recollection of Various Muscular Acts," *Am. J. Physiol.*, 94 (1):22–34, July 1930.

1930   3. "Visual Imagination and Recollection," *Am. J. Physiol.*, 95 (3):694–702, December 1930.

1930   4. "Evidence of Contraction of Specific Muscles During Imagination," *Am. J. Physiol.*, 95 (3):703–712, December 1930.

1931   5. "Variation of Specific Muscles Contracting During Imagination," *Am. J. Physiol.*, 96 (1):115–121, January 1931.

1931   6. "A Note on Mental Activities Concerning an Amputated Limb," *Am. J. Physiol.*, 96 (1):122–125, January 1931.

1931   7. "Imagination, Recollection and Abstract Thinking Involving the Speech Musculature," *Am. J. Physiol.*, 97 (1):200–209, April 1931.

1932 "Indications for Progressive Relaxation in the Practice of Medicine and the Technic of Progressive Relaxation" in *Principles and Practices of Physical Therapy*, Ed. H. E. Mock, R. Pemberton and J. S. Coulter, W. F. Prior Co., Hagerstown, Maryland, Vol. I, Chap. 12, 1932.

1932 "Electrophysiology of Mental Activities," *Am. J. Psychol.*, 44:677–694, October 1932.

1933 "Measurement of the Action-potentials in the Peripheral Nerves of Man without Anesthetic," *Proc. Soc. Exp. Biol. & Med.*, 30:713–715, 1933.

1934 "Electrical Measurement of Activities in Nerve and Muscle," from *The Problem of Mental Disorder*, pp. 133–145, McGraw-Hill Book Company, Inc., New York, 1934.

1934 "Electrical Measurements Concerning Muscular Contraction (Tonus) and the Cultivation of Relaxation in Man, Studies on Arm Flexors," *Am. J. Physiol.*, 107 (1):230–248, January 1934.

1934 "Electrical Measurements Concerning Muscular Contraction (Tonus) and the Cultivation of Relaxation in Man—Relaxation-times of Individuals," *Am. J. Physiol.*, 108 (3):573–580, June 1934.

1936 "The Course of Relaxation in Muscles of Athletes," *Am. J. Psychol.*, 48:98–108, January 1936.

1939 "The Neurovoltmeter," *Am. J. Psychol.*, 52:620–624, October 1939.

1939 "Electrical and Mechanical Activity of the Human Non-Pregnant Uterus," Jacobson, E., Julius E. Lackner, Melvin B. Sinykin, *Am. J. Obst. & Gynec.*, 38:1008–1021, December 1939.

1939 1. "Variation of Blood Pressure with Skeletal Muscle Tension and Relaxation," *Ann. Internal Med.*, 12 (8):1194–1212, February 1939.

1939 "Variations in Blood Pressure with Skeletal Muscle Tension (Action-potentials) in Man."
2. "The Influence of Brief Voluntary Contractions," *Am. J. Physiol.*, 126 (3):546–547, July 1939.

1940 "Variation of Blood Pressure with Skeletal Muscle Tension and Relaxation."
3. "The Heart Beat," *Ann. Internal Med.*, 13 (9):1619–1625, March 1940.

1940 4. "Variation of Blood Pressure with Brief Voluntary Muscular Contractions," *J. Lab. & Clin. Med.*, 25 (10):1029–1037, July 1940.

1940 "Cultivated Relaxation in 'Essential' Hypertension," *Arch. Phys. Therapy*, 21:645–654, November 1940.

1940 "The Direct Measurement of Nervous and Muscular States with the Integrating Neurovoltmeter (Action-potential Integrator)," *Am. J. Psychiat.*, 97 (3):513–523, November 1940.

1940 "An Integrating Voltmeter for the Study of Nerve and Muscle Potentials," *Rev. Sci. Instr.*, 11 (12):415–418, December 1940.

1940 *The Principles and Practice of Physical Therapy*, rev. ed., Vol. 1, Chap. 12; Vol. 3, Chap. 18, W. F. Prior Co., Hagerstown, 1940.

1940 Jacobson, E., J. E. Lackner and M. B. Sinykin, "Activity of the Human Non-pregnant Uterus," *Am. J. Psychol.*, 53 (3):407–417, July 1940.

"Educational Relaxation for the Classroom Teacher," *Education*, December 1940.

1941 "Recording Action-potentials without Photography," *Am. J. Psychol.*, 54:266–269, April 1941.

1941 "The Physiological Conception and Treatment of Certain Common 'Psychoneuroses,'" *Am. J. Psychiat.*, 98 (2):219–226, September 1941.

"The Window Proctoscope," *Rev. Gastroenterol*, 8:315–316, July–August 1941.

1942 "The Effect of Daily Rest without Training to Relax on Muscular Tonus," *Am. J. Psychol.*, 55:248–254, April 1942.

1942 Jacobson, E., and F. L. Kraft, "Contraction Potentials (Right Quadriceps Femoris) in Man During Reading," *Am. J. Physiol.*, 137 (1):1–5, August 1942.

1943 "Innervation and 'Tonus' of Striated Muscle in Man," *J. Nervous & Mental Disease*, 97 (2):197–203, February 1943.

1943 "Cultivated Relaxation for the Elimination of 'Nervous Breakdowns'," *Arch. Phys. Therapy*, 24:133–143, 176, March 1943.

1943   "'Tonus' in Striated Muscle," *Am. J. Psychol.*, 56:433–437, July 1943.

1943   "Rest: Physical and Mental," *Illinois Med. J.*, 84:2, August 1943.

1943   "Muscular Tension and the Smoking of Cigarettes," *Am. J. Psychol.*, 56:559–574, October 1943.

1943   "The Cultivation of Physiological Relaxation," *Am. Internal Med.*, 19 (6):965–972, December 1943.

1944   "Direct Measurements of the Effects of Bromides, Sodium Amytal and of Caffeine in Man," *Ann. Internal Med.*, 21 (3):455–468, September 1944.

        "Rest: Physical & Mental," in *Medical Physics*, Ed. Otto Glassner, Yearbook Publishers, Chicago, Vol. I, pp. 1239–1241.

1946   "Electrical Measurements of Mental Activities in Man," *Trans. N.Y. Acad. Sci.* (2) (8):272–273, June 1946.

1947   "The Influence of Relaxation upon the Blood Pressure in 'Essential Hypertension'," *Fed. Proc.*, 6 (1): March 1947.

1948   "Theory of Essential Hypertension in Man," *Trans. N.Y. Acad. Sci.* (2) 11 (2):49–50, December 1948.

1950   "Supplement to Rest: Physical and Mental," *Med. Phys.*, Vol. 2, 1950.

1951   "Muscular Tension and the Estimation of Effort," *Am. J. Psychol.*, 64:112–117, January 1951.

        "A Rejoiner," *Am. J. Psychol.*, 64:122–124 January 1951.

1952   "Specialized Electromyography in Supplement to Clinical Observations During Hyperkinetic States in Man ('Functional Nervous Conditions')," *Fed. Proc.*, 11 (1): March 1952.

1953   "Principles Underlying Coronary Heart Disease (Considerations for a Working Hypothesis)," *Cardiologia*, 26:83, 1955, read before the Am. Assoc. Advance. Sci., Boston, December 1953.

1955 "Neuromuscular Controls in Man: Methods of Self-Direction in Health and in Disease," *Am. J. Psychol.*, 68:549–561, December 1955.

1958 "Physiological Psychiatry. Basis and Working Principles for a Science of Psychiatry."

1970 "Psychology and the Integrative Action of the Nervous System," *Acta Symbolica*, Vol. I, No. 2, 31–35, 1970.

1971 "New Concepts of (1) Anxiety and (2) Mental Activity," *Acta Symbolica*, Vol. II, No. 2, 28–33, 1971.

"Neuromuscular Activity in Man: Sampling in 30-Min. Test Periods with Integrating Neurovoltmeter and Digital Computer," Edmund Jacobson and Richard E. Lange, Proceedings of the International Union of Physiological Sciences, Vol. IX, 1971.

1972 October, Invited address, Biofeedback Society, Boston, Massachusetts.

1973 May 24, Invited address, Western Pennsylvania Heart Association, "Early Hypertension and Coronary Heart Disease Treated by Progressive Relaxation."

THE PSYCHOPHYSIOLOGY OF THINKING, Studies of Covert Processes, Edited by F. J. McGuigan and R. A. Schoonover-Academic Press

"TO DR. EDMUND JACOBSON, In recognition of his pioneering research in the psychophysiology of higher mental processes."

1974 July 8–12, Class instruction on tension control, U.C.L.A.

1975 June 6–10, Workshop on Progressive Relaxation with Professor F. J. McGuigan.

October 9, "Grand Lecture", Temple University, Philadelphia, "The Variable Teaching of Progressive Relaxation."

October 10, Workshop, "How To Teach the Beginnings of Technique in Progressive Relaxation."

October 25, 26. Address on Tension Control, The American Association for the Advancement of Tension Control, Chicago, Professor F. J. McGuigan, Executive Director.

Together with Richard E. Lange perfected a previously engineered portable model of the Jacobson integrating neurovoltmeter, attaining the most electronic measurement accuracy of any instrument up to date.

1976　Series of articles in press and in preparation on energy expenditures per minute in human subjects lying prone. These include healthy "norms" as well as patients under progressive relaxation treatment for various conditions including essential hypertension, with and without the use of medications.

Some Related Publications by Professional Teachers

1926　"Changes in the Response to Electrical Shock by Varying Muscular Conditions," M. Miller, *Jour. Exper. Psychol.*, IX, 26–44, 1926.

1951　"Relaxation Methods in U.S. Navy Air Schools," Commander William Neufeld, U.S.N.R., *Am. J. Psychiatry.*, Vol. 108, No. 2, August 1951.

1958　*A Therapy for Anxiety Tension Reactions*, Haugen, G. B., Dixon, H. H., And Dickel, H. A., Macmillan, 1958.

1966　"Use of Jacobson's Methods in Different Fields of Medicine in Connection with a Case," E. Szirmai, *Agressologie*, Vol. VII, No. 6, 641–645, June 6, 1966.

INDEX